Madoff's Other Secret

Madoff's Other Secret

Love, Money, Bernie, and Me

Sheryl Weinstein

ST. MARTIN'S PRESS 🐟 NEW YORK

www.stmartins.com

ISBN 978-0-312-61837-7

First Edition: August 2009

10 9 8 7 6 5 4 3 2 1

To the tens of thousands of honest, innocent, and unsuspecting investors worldwide who share with me and understand only too well the horror of being financially and emotionally decimated. I look forward to the day when we all will be able to put this behind us; find peace, resolution, and restitution and once again enjoy our families, friends, and lives. Although he has stolen our money, we will not allow him to rob us of our self-worth, happiness, or futures.

Acknowledgments

I have made some new and special friends during this arduous writing process. To Lisa Pulitzer, I don't think I could have survived the last two months without you right there by my side. I felt an instant bond from our first hug. Not only are you a most gifted writer, but more important, you are a thoroughly amazing person. Even under tremendous pressure, you have never shown even a bit of impatience, intolerance, or annoyance. I look forward to having you in my life.

To Sally Richardson, publisher, you have become an oasis of calmness, sanity, and safety in my life, and for that I will be forever grateful.

To Erin Casey, without you, there might never have been a proposal for my story. You gave it the voice—my voice—as well as life. I'm sorry that you didn't live closer so that you could be there not only for the beginning, but for the end as well. I thoroughly enjoyed working with you and look forward to meeting you and giving you a big hug in person one day soon.

What I regret most is having to involve my husband and son in my story—but they are such important parts of my life. It is also unfortunate that this story focuses on probably the worst years of our marriage. Since that time we have learned to live with greater respect and admiration for each other. Frankly, I don't know how I would feel if the situation were reversed. I do know that he has been there for me 110 percent, and I am so very, very grateful for his love, support, and understanding.

To my husband and partner, Ronnie, I know your love has always been there for me. Since I am incapable of changing the past and the worst is hopefully behind us, together let's look toward our newly revised future. You know how much I love you.

To my son, Eric, my "little guy," without whom I would never have experienced the depths and range of emotions that accompany those of total unqualified love and adoration—always know that your mommy loves you.

To my parents, Edith and Murray Wasserman, I thank you both for instilling in me your values and work ethics. I keep your pictures on my bedside table so that you're there in my thoughts at night before I go to sleep.

To my grandma Fannie—I have never stopped missing you. During my loneliest moments I have wrapped your love around me to help keep me warm. Grandpa Sam, I'm sorry that Alzheimer's prevented me from knowing you as you once were.

To Aunt Ida and Uncle Marvin, you truly were my other parents in every sense of the word. Robbie, you will always be my "totie."

Acknowledgments

And to my unknown relative from whom I inherited my memory gene, I am forever grateful.

Ronnie and I learned about the importance of friends during this difficult time. We would like to extend our deepest gratitude and love to our friends, who not only gave us their emotional support, but also offered monetary help. (You know who you are.) Please know that we will never forget your generosity in our darkest hours. We were relieved not to have to take you up on your offers, but want you to know that you will always hold a very special place in our hearts.

Madoff's Other Secret

Prologue

For almost three months after Bernie Madoff was arrested, I wandered through life in a mental fog. Day after day, I awoke with a weight on me; this total feeling of dread. I couldn't think about anything else and, in fact, I'm still looking forward to the day when I actually don't think about what Bernie has done to our lives. I don't believe that day will ever come. But I remain hopeful. Not only do I feel like Bernie stole our money, but he also stole our future dreams, a part of my son's future, the little money my parents had left me, and the money my eighty-eight-year-old mother-in-law had given to us to invest for her.

When news of Bernie's fraud first broke, my husband, Ronnie, and I kept our loss a secret. We spoke about it with very few friends, only those who already knew that we had our money with Bernie's firm. To me there was a feeling of shame and embarrassment attached to being a victim as well as loss of pride, which is the other side of the same coin. There's a piece that makes you feel as though you're being punished for something you did wrong. I didn't want anybody to know. Neither of us did. And we also realized that we would have to sell our apartment and didn't want potential buyers to know how precarious our financial situation was or how vulnerable we were.

In those early days, my dark, ironic humor took hold. One night as I sat in my bedroom, unable to comprehend all that had happened, a thought entered my mind: *I am probably the only person in the world who was screwed twice by Bernie Madoff.* At first, I could only think about all the money we'd lost. The double sense of betrayal didn't strike me right away. I couldn't really, truly get my arms around it or believe it.

That first night, my son, Eric, joined us in our apartment. He owned a one-bedroom apartment a few floors below us in the same building. The scene was surreal. The three of us sat in the living room, sipping wine and trying to make sense of what Bernie had done. I felt responsible. Investing our money had been my job. Financial matters had always been left up to me. I had insisted that Eric keep his investment and pension funds with Bernie. It had been my idea four years ago to refinance our apartment and give Bernie the cash. Even though Ronnie had understood and agreed to it, I still felt it was my responsibility. And later on when I felt compelled to

level with my husband and my son about the double nature of my relationship with Bernie, you can only imagine
that my sense of responsibility was almost too great to
bear.

Over the course of the evening, our phone rang several
times. Friends who were aware of our investment with
Bernie were checking in to see if we were okay. I was
grateful for their concern: in my mind I couldn't help
feeling they were secretly relieved that it wasn't them.
Over the years, many of our friends had inquired about
getting into Bernie's fund. I'd asked Bernie a while back
about bringing in a friend or two. At that time, he'd told
me that the fund was "closed." I am so grateful that was
the case. I can't imagine how I would feel knowing I was
responsible for their losses as well as our own.

We didn't stay up very late that night. I took an anti-
anxiety drug and a sleeping pill and went to bed early.
Sleep was my only escape to avoid dealing with the
reality and the horror of it all. I kept listening to the
television, waiting for the newscasters to come on and
report it had been one big mistake. There hasn't been a
morning I haven't Googled "Madoff" to see the latest
news.

He had stolen all of our money and still I couldn't feel
hatred—hatred is a very draining emotion and I needed
all of my strength to keep myself and my life and family
together. What do you do with twenty years of feelings
and memories? They just don't disappear overnight.

Ronnie wasn't aware of my entire story until mid-January. I had begun speaking to people confidentially about writing a book and I worried that my story would get around or show up on the gossip page of one of the major newspapers one morning. I decided it was best to tell him before that happened. I had faith that Ronnie's reaction would be all right. I felt comfortable being truthful with him. I wasn't proud of what I had done but we had been married for almost thirty-seven years and this was the extent of my unfaithfulness. There were no other ghosts in my closet.

We sat down after dinner one night. I told him that I had something to share with him. I said that it was going to be a one-way conversation and I didn't want him to share with me anything that may have happened in his life. How much sharing could one marriage take?

Before he could say anything I plunged in. "I had an affair fifteen years ago."

He didn't appear shocked or angry but he asked, "With whom?"

This was the hard part. "With Bernie," I said.

"You're kidding!" He almost laughed. "With Bernie? Him? What about Joey?"

Joey was my college boyfriend, and someone I'd stayed in touch with over the years.

"What about Joey?" I asked.

"I thought if you were going to have an affair with anyone it would be him," Ronnie said.

"No, it was Bernie."

I told my son, Eric, a week later. He was loving and supportive. "Yes, Dad had issues back then, didn't he?"

In order to move forward, I decided to tell my story. I truly hope Ronnie will be able to forgive me for sharing these private moments in our lives.

Part One

Chapter One

It was nine A.M. on February 25, 1988, when I stepped out of the cab in front of the red-enameled granite-and-steel building at 885 Third Avenue and pushed my way into the glistening, glass-enclosed lobby. It was New York's famed Lipstick Building, the name given to the thirty-four-story East Side skyscraper that stretches between Fifty-third and Fifty-fourth streets.

Since its completion two years earlier, the three-tiered, ultramodern structure had drawn many admirers. They viewed its curves and jazzy red hue as a welcome contrast to the black-and-white, sharp-edged design of its neighbor the Citicorp Center. Lipstick Building designers John Burgee and Philip Johnson were being hailed for the building's sleek, elliptical lines and its unusual egg-shaped lobby. The lobby soared two stories high and incorporated a pedestrian walkway. The structure was so fanciful and pleasing, it would have been hard to imagine anything so apocalyptic could be percolating within its walls.

I was curious to check it out for myself and set off toward the bank of elevators in the lobby. The much-touted Toscana Restaurant occupied a large chunk on the Fifty-fourth Street side. I would just take a quick peek inside, not wanting to be late for my 9:15 meeting on the eighteenth floor with the principal of the brokerage house that bore his name.

As chief financial officer of Hadassah, a Jewish charitable organization of 350,000-plus women, I'd been asked to accompany three of our executive volunteers to a meeting to discuss the logistics of a donation. It wasn't part of my typical agenda, but this was no ordinary transaction.

The donor, an elderly man named Albert I., lived in France, and wanted to remain anonymous. He'd earmarked $7 million to fund a specialized medical facility to be founded by one of our doctors. The only caveats to the donation, at the time the largest Hadassah had received from a single benefactor, were that the money be used to support the facility and that a New York broker named Bernard Madoff manage the funds.

This was the first time we'd had a donor stipulate how the monies were to be held and invested. Normally, they would just be given directly to Hadassah. The request was a bit unusual, but it made sense. It was a large sum, and if managed properly it could grow even as it funded Hadassah's work. Mr. Madoff was to disburse the funds as they were needed. In the office, we referred to Albert I. as our "French connection."

I was already on my third piece of Nicorette when I heard our president, Ruth P., calling to me from across the lobby. I had stopped smoking more than a year ago and was still using the gum to pacify my urge to light up. I wasn't sure if I'd be successful at quitting smoking for good, since I'd already failed twice before. I'd promised my son I'd give it another try after he came home from school in tears. His teacher had given a presentation about the dangers of smoking, and he was convinced I was going to die. I made a personal "reverse psychological" pact with myself that if I failed this time, I would never try to quit again. To this day, twenty-three years later, I have never smoked another cigarette.

Hastening past a colonnade of granite pillars, my heels clicking on the polished granite floors, I arrived at the bank of elevators, where Ruth and the others were waiting. Our treasurer, Debbie K., and Bernice T., chairwoman of Hadassah International, greeted me as I fought to catch my breath. Bernice was the one who'd made the initial contact with our donor during a trip to Paris. She wanted to be at the meeting to finalize the transaction and meet the man who would be managing the funds.

None of us at Hadassah had ever heard of Bernard Madoff or his firm, Bernard L. Madoff Investment Securities. Apparently, our donor had met him through a personal introduction some years back. We were all a bit surprised that the donor was declining even the smallest recognition: no honorary plaque, no commemorative inscription, not even a framed certificate of thanks. While it struck me as odd, it didn't raise any red flags, although now in retrospect, I wish I had asked more questions about his desire for anonymity.

I was already rummaging around in my purse for another piece of Nicorette when the elevator doors opened onto the eighteenth floor. The offices were contemporary and stark with glass walls that served as partitions dividing the space. The color scheme was masculine, black and silver right down to the financial prospectus and other printed materials in the reception area. We were led to a windowed conference room with a fabulous city panorama.

"Please wait here, Mr. Madoff will be right with you," the receptionist instructed.

I knew from past meetings that Ruth didn't like to sit with her back to a door, so I waited for her to get situated at the conference table, then I sat down directly across from her. This way, I could pick up any nonverbal cues she might telegraph during our meeting and still enjoy the Manhattan skyline beyond the sparkling double-paned windows.

We had been in the conference room about five minutes when I sensed footsteps in the hallway behind me. I didn't see Mr. Madoff when he first entered the room, but I watched as Ruth's eyes widened, her thin lips parting in a contented grin. Turning to look, I observed that he was wearing a cardigan. His casual attire seemed contrived in its subtlety, as if to say, *I'm relaxed and in control; trust me!* It was one of the only times I would ever see him so casually dressed.

"Hello, ladies. I'm Bernie Madoff," he said, striding to the head of the conference table, where he stopped, placed his hands on the table, leaned forward slightly, and nodded his head in greeting.

When his gaze fell on me, he blinked and looked a bit surprised. I'm sure he was expecting a group of elderly Jewish women, and I was certainly an exception to the case. At thirty-nine, I was younger than my colleagues by more than two decades. He gave me a welcoming smile, a smile I'll never forget. It wasn't lewd and lascivious, but slightly seductive and almost happy. I knew instantly that he was attracted to me.

Though I'd felt an instant surge of connection, I wasn't particularly attracted to him—he didn't have the pretty-boy features I preferred. Still, there was something in him that piqued my interest.

A few minutes into the meeting Bernie had to step out to take a call. As soon as the door closed behind him, the women at the table began making comments. "I had no idea he would be so good-looking," one said.

I was a little surprised by their remarks. I didn't find him particularly handsome. What I was reacting to went much deeper. My female intuition was telling me there was something else going on with this man; there was an intrinsic sensuality about him that was both attractive and alluring. Yet there was also an oily slickness that I found disconcerting. When the meeting continued, Bernie kept catching my eye in a way that was different from how he looked at the other women in the room. And when he wasn't looking at me, I found myself admiring his distinctive profile.

Before the end of our first meeting, Bernie and I had exchanged business cards. As the caretaker of Hadassah's finances, I would have to speak with him occasionally to discuss how the funds were being invested. But I also knew Bernie would be calling me regardless. Women have a way of sensing these things, so I wasn't surprised when a few days later he phoned my office to let me know that the donation had been transferred.

"Albert has deposited the money," he said. "Would you like to get together and discuss investment strategies?"

"Of course," I replied.

"Why don't you come over and have lunch at my office? We'll talk about it then."

Chapter Two

When I arrived at Bernie's office, I was again escorted to the conference room. The table was set for lunch. Two place settings were arranged with contemporary glassware and china. In the few minutes I waited for Bernie to join me, I wondered if I would experience that same powerful connection I'd felt during our first meeting. Looking out over the city, I thought about how nice it felt to be noticed by a man, especially one as influential and successful as Bernie.

I'd been married for sixteen years, and still I'd felt alone a long time. My husband, Ronnie, could be a difficult man. He had a temper and suffered from significant mood swings. One minute he'd be on top of the world, and the next he'd be raging over something minor and certainly not worthy of a knock-down, drag-out battle.

Ronnie was a contradiction. An all-around partner, he cleaned and cooked, and not a day went by when he didn't bring me coffee in bed. He was also a consummate parent to our son, Eric. When Eric was young, Ronnie would spend hours on end playing games with him. In the morning, he was up early preparing breakfast. There were never any lumps in Eric's Cream of Wheat. He had the cleanest ears in New York City. When I was traveling with Hadassah, Ronnie would drop him off at school and get him ready for sleepaway camp.

On the surface, Ronnie was engaging and personable. People who didn't really know him thought he was a very easygoing guy. However, those near and dear to him had seen his "dark side." A lot of anger would surface if he felt he had lost control. He liked order and neatness. If Eric didn't put his things away, Ronnie would lose patience and become annoyed.

When he felt pressured, he would take it out on me. I was the perfect scapegoat. For years, I had tried and failed to reduce his stress by taking responsibility for our finances, our marriage, and the everyday necessities. I tried to avoid pushing the buttons that sent him over the edge, but my attempts to calm him were becoming less and less effective and more and more exhausting.

I became aware of Ronnie's mercurial behavior even before we were married. It made itself evident after only a few months of dating. Ronnie's mood swings were often unpredictable. He would change from a smiling, sweet guy to a scowling, furious one in a heartbeat. The first time it happened we were out at a club dancing and I got tired and walked off the dance floor without giving him sufficient notice. Ronnie became angry, feeling that I had made him look silly. He was extremely sensitive and easily upset.

Another time, we went skiing. I was a novice skier and felt nervous as I approached the mountain. Ronnie, on the other hand, was an excellent skier. Having attended the University of Denver, he'd had plenty of practice. As he traversed the slopes, he was the picture of grace and fluidity. We were on the beginner slope as he attempted to coax me down the hill. I was trying to snowplow but couldn't stop and ended up plowing right into him, knocking him down. He was furious, feeling that I had made him look ridiculous. He skied away in a huff.

Later that evening, we were in the lodge playing Ping-Pong and I mentioned that I had been a fabulous player in college. It was New Year's Eve. I was in a long dress when he challenged me to a game. I think we played fifteen or sixteen rounds. When I told him I was exhausted, he got mad, making me play until he finally won.

In order to cope with the stress of my marriage, I distanced myself from Ronnie spiritually and emotionally. I had built a successful career that allowed me to travel and have a life of my own. Throughout the years, I carried on a pseudoemotional relationship with my old college boyfriend, Joey. I would see him periodically because, unlike with my husband, I was able to confide in him about the distress I was experiencing in my life. He made me feel good, and there was a part of me that wanted to resume our relationship. But I was too frightened because of our history.

I was eighteen and a virgin when I met Joey during the second semester of my freshman year at New York State University at Buffalo. It was the six-month anniversary of my grandmother's death. She'd been diagnosed with cancer the previous year, and died two days before I left to go to college.

I was still in mourning that March day in 1967 when I met Joey. I'd gotten spruced up a bit to lift my spirits and Joey noticed immediately. He was one year ahead of me and ranked at the top of his class at the university's business school. He was very, very thin, something I before had never found particularly attractive. In high school, I'd always dated well-built football hunks.

It was mostly Joey's extroverted personality that attracted me. He was an avid reader who loved stimulating conversation and a good debate. He was an intellectual shark, always looking for something new to learn. Being with him was never boring. On our first date, he told me we could never marry. He was a Syrian Jew, and had to marry within his community. I was an Ashkenazi Jew. His parents would not have approved. I didn't take him seriously. I thought it was just a silly line. We dated for more than a year, often sleeping together in the same bed. There was petting but no oral sex or intercourse. I simply wasn't emotionally prepared to take the big step.

We had been dating for more than a year before we finally had sex, and we'd been sleeping together for a couple of years before I had my first orgasm. I thought it felt really great, but I was so naive, I didn't realize what had happened.

As strange as this may seem, it wasn't until after we broke up that I discovered the art of masturbating to climax.

Giving up my virginity was special. I felt totally connected to Joey emotionally and physically, and I believed that we would eventually be married. That commitment made me feel incredibly vulnerable. I don't think Joey understood how hurtful it was when he disappeared without a word for days or weeks at a time. I'd call around looking for him, terrified that something dreadful had happened. The first time he went missing in action we were home for summer break. I thought I would be seeing a lot of him even though I was on Long Island and he was in Brooklyn for the summer. One night, he took me to New York City. It was my first official city date. We dined at Toots Shor's and then went to the Copacabana. When I excused myself to use the ladies' room, Joey handed me a dollar to tip the attendant. I had rarely been to Manhattan, and I knew nothing about attended ladies' rooms. He was opening up a whole new world for me, one I fell in love with for the rest of my life.

For the next couple of weeks, we would see each other, and then one day he called to say I'd left my jacket in his car. He was going to drive it out to me on Long Island. I was excited to see him, and when he arrived I answered the door eagerly. He told me he was going away to San

Francisco for the rest of the summer. I was all of eighteen and heartbroken. Suddenly I realized that this was his way of breaking up with me without really doing it. I felt as though my world had just collapsed around me as I stood in the darkness of my bedroom watching out the window as a mysterious female passenger reached over and gave him a big hug and kiss.

Joey and I ran into each other on campus when we returned to college in the fall, and by December our relationship was back on. Our on-again, off-again love affair stretched over almost four years, with similar dramas unfolding along the way. Every time I felt we were getting closer, something would happen or a new girl would show up. In retrospect, Joey's commitment and intimacy issues were partly the cause of his escapist mentality. Perhaps he was trying to accommodate his parents' wish that he marry a Syrian Jew. All of this explained his long and painful absences. But back then, I felt responsible and was always trying to "fix everything," believing there was something wrong with me. I ended up transferring to New York University in my junior year to be with him after learning he was not returning to college in Buffalo. I didn't know it at the time, but he had to be in New York to address draft-related issues. It was the middle of the Vietnam War and young men were being drafted. As was his usual modus operandi, he'd waited until the night before I was scheduled to leave for fall semester to tell me he'd transferred to a school in New York. I was inconsolable.

By the time I met Ronnie, I felt like damaged goods.

In my quest to feel better, I'd gone to a hospital clinic. I wanted to see a therapist. I was interviewed by a resident. He asked a number of very intimate and personal questions about me and my sexual experiences. He told me that the hospital office would get back to me with a referral to see one of its doctors. A few days later, he called to ask me out on a date. I felt violated. I'd gone for help and I ended up feeling violated. I told him no and eventually wrote a letter of complaint to the hospital.

It was the summer of 1970, and Joey had once again disappeared. Our friend Harold H. had told me he'd gone to Boston. After living for a time at the 92nd Street Y, I had just moved into my first apartment. It was on Eightieth Street and First Avenue, and I shared it with three roommates. I agreed to accompany one of them to a singles bar on First Avenue, hoping to run into Joey. The whole of First Avenue between Sixty-first and Sixty-fourth streets was lined with restaurants such as Maxwell's Plum, Friday's, and Proof of the Pudding. They all had extensive bar areas where singles could congregate, listen to music, and knock back a drink.

We decided to go to Mr. Laffs, a sports bar owned by two professional baseball players from the Yankees and the Mets. The owners would sometimes buy us drinks and have us sit in the window, no doubt to attract male customers. We'd been there only a few minutes when I spotted Ronnie sitting at the end of the bar. He was stunning: six foot one, athletic, and deeply tanned. I walked over and ordered a Coke, my drink of choice back then.

We smiled at each other. We kept looking at each other, but he didn't make any overtures toward me. After a while, I got tired of waiting and went outside to socialize with friends on the sidewalk. I had been out there a few minutes when Ronnie finally emerged. It wasn't until some time later that he admitted it had taken him that long to find the courage to speak to me.

When Joey finally returned to New York that summer, I told him I'd met someone else. There was never a final resolution. During my relationship with Joey I experienced the beginnings of an ulcer, migraine headaches, and a spastic colon, all of which went away when I stopped dating him. I believe these symptoms were the result of internalizing my feeling of humiliation. We continued to speak. Once, he and Ronnie turned up in the lobby of my apartment building at the same time. I came downstairs to find them both standing there. Joey later commented on Ronnie's good looks. I think he was thoroughly intimidated.

But I knew I had to move on from Joey, and in all other respects Ronnie was everything I wanted in a boyfriend. He was handsome and charismatic, and he made me feel secure. I knew he would be there on Saturday night, and he treated me with the utmost respect. More important, the world would see there couldn't possibly be anything wrong with me because I was with someone so attractive. No one could see I was damaged goods when I was with Ronnie. Soon Ronnie and I were practically living together. It had gotten to the point where I returned to my apartment only every four weeks to take my turn tidying up. My roommates referred to me as the "cleaning girl."

I never felt humiliated with Ronnie in the same way that I had with Joey. He came home every night; he gave me his paycheck. He was there, he married me, he didn't disappear on me. But Ronnie, like all of us, had warts, too. His chronic irritability took a big toll on me, not so much in the early years of our marriage because we can tolerate more when we're young, but as time passed it got worse. I always felt he was unhappy with me; he was so critical. Everything I did seemed to annoy him. By the time I met Bernie, I had endured years of emotional abuse. It was verbal abuse, but there was always a latent possibility that it would become physical. Ronnie is a tall man, and his height intimidated me. He'd tower over me and rage, screaming and yelling and getting in my face. I was increasingly thinking about leaving him. Financially, I was at a point where I could finally make it happen.

My emotional affair with Joey had provided some relief. I think if he had initiated another physical affair, I might have found the courage to leave Ronnie. But I'll never know. Joey's previous emotional effect on me frightened me too much to go there. I believe subconsciously I was looking for a way out. One of my shrinks told me that people find it easier to leave when there is somebody else in the picture. Few leave a dysfunctional marriage to be alone. Joey had recently gotten remarried. He told me that being with me had made it impossible to be married to a Syrian girl, after all. At just shy of forty, I was still longing for kind male companionship.

Enter Bernie Madoff.

I was lost in thought and jumped when I heard Bernie's voice behind me.

"Hi, Sheryl," he said in a low, husky tone.

Turning from the window, I watched as he gracefully crossed the conference room to greet me. Immediately, I knew I hadn't imagined his attraction for me. That same wide, desire-filled smile spread across his face, and an air of excitement saturated the room. This time, he was wearing a navy suit with a light blue shirt that made his gray-blue eyes more alluring than I remembered. When I reached out to shake his hand, he simply took it and leaned in to kiss my cheek. "So glad you could come today."

We sat at one end of the large table: Bernie took his place at the head, and I sat to his right so that I could enjoy the city views. Behind me was the glass wall that looked out into an office area.

For our lunch, Bernie had catered sandwiches from the Quilted Giraffe on Madison Avenue, which, though they were delicious, posed a real problem for me. Bernie raised his eyebrows as I set the bread aside. After a couple of bites, I felt the need to explain. My son's Bar Mitzvah was coming up in a few weeks, and I had been on a low-carbohydrate diet for as long as I could remember. I wasn't heavy, but I was eager to drop a few pounds.

"You don't look like you need to be on any type of diet to me," he said, and grinned. "You're perfect!" I could feel myself blush. I hadn't dated for years and was unaccustomed to having men give me more than a superficial compliment. It was both flattering and alarming. A rich, powerful, older man with beautiful blue eyes was taking notice of me. What I didn't realize was that behind those blue eyes was a hidden agenda. Was he seducing me, using the charitable donation as the basis for continued contact? Bernie Madoff, the ultimate schemer.

"Thank you." I returned my focus to the sandwiches. I was relieved when Bernie shifted the conversation back to my plans for Eric's Bar Mitzvah. As we talked and ate, I couldn't help but notice that Bernie chomped while eating his sandwich. He had fine table manners other than the lip smacking.

Throughout our lunch meeting we talked very little business. We discussed our beloved city, and Bernie talked a lot about his family. A few years before, he and his wife, Ruth, had moved to Manhattan from Roslyn, Long Island, and were enjoying the many opportunities the city had to offer.

Bernie grew up a middle-class kid from Queens and met Ruth when she was thirteen years old and he was sixteen. By the time he and I met, the high school sweethearts had been married almost thirty years. Bernie was approaching his fiftieth birthday. He explained that his wife; his brother, Peter; and his older son, Mark, were in business with him. His younger son, Andrew, would be graduating from the Wharton School of the University of Pennsylvania in the spring with a degree in economics and was expected to join the firm.

"Oh, Wharton, that's where I completed my accounting courses," I said. "My husband and I were living in Philadelphia at the time."

Bernie asked me how long I'd been with Hadassah, and told me his firm had been in the Lipstick Building since its completion two years earlier. I was enjoying our conversation and having a wonderful time. We discovered many common interests, including a love of movies, restaurants, and the theater. I remember laughing a lot with Bernie that day.

At the end of our lunch, we still hadn't talked about investment strategy. The one bit of business we had discussed briefly was whether he'd be willing to invest some of Hadassah's money in addition to Albert's donation. Bernie agreed that it would be a possibility, and I told him I'd run the idea by our volunteers.

"Lunch was lovely, Bernie."

"My pleasure. Next time I'll try to offer something you'll find more appealing."

"It was fine, really. Diets don't last forever," I said, smiling.

He walked me to the elevator and kissed my cheek once more as we said good-bye.

"I'll be in touch," he said.

As I got into a cab to return to my office, I felt eighteen

again. Our time together had felt like a first date. It was comfortable, yet provocative and flirtatious.

A few days later, Bernie called my office, and I was surprised by how happy I was to hear from him.

"How's your diet coming along?" he said, chuckling. The huskiness in his voice was a welcome sound.

"Very well, thanks."

"I'm sure you'll look amazing. Eric will have the best-looking mother at the party."

He spoke in a soft, sexy voice, and I felt heat prickle my face. "Thank you. Listen, I spoke with the volunteers and our treasurer. We'd like to have you invest some of Hadassah's money."

"No problem. Why don't you come by my office late tomorrow afternoon? Since we didn't get around to it last time, I'll explain our investment strategy. Afterward, perhaps we'll have time for a drink?"

I agreed without hesitation. "I'll see you tomorrow, then, about five o'clock."

Chapter Three

That week, I had called our broker at Prudential Bache to find out more about Bernie Madoff. It was something I routinely did when someone new was doing business with Hadassah. But in this case it wasn't urgent because his involvement was at the request of our donor. Still, I was intrigued. There was an element of mystery about him. I was looking forward to seeing him again. It was a new adventure, something to spice up my day.

It was late afternoon when I arrived at the Lipstick Building for the third time. I'd wanted to look my best and had worn my favorite pink suit to work. Since joining Hadassah in 1984, I'd been filling my closet with the warm colors I adored. It was liberating to be free of the black and gray suits of my corporate past. I tended to be conservative in my dress, favoring Dana Buchman and Ellen Tracy suits, high heels, and the few pieces of jewelry that had been handed down in my family. After nearly a decade in the business world, I could finally be myself in this job.

In my prior position as controller of New York City's famed Lincoln Center, the environment was both corporate and political. As a woman, I had to fight hard to prove my worth. I had been assistant controller for about six months when the title of controller was offered to me. It was a high-profile job with a great deal of visibility. I was the first woman to achieve the position. I viewed it as yet another breakthrough in the fight to break the glass ceiling—until I became privy to what had been said during a highly confidential meeting.

I was tremendously upset when I heard that a senior board member was opposed to my promotion. He had commented that a woman "could not" have the title of controller of Lincoln Center. It was the early 1980s, and sexism in the workplace was rampant. Ultimately, I did receive the promotion and the title of controller, but simultaneously they hired a man to be the director of finance. Still, I was responsible for the accounting functions of the entire facility and had twenty people reporting to me.

I had been at Lincoln Center for two years when Hadassah approached me. I'd been recommended through my old accounting firm, Peat Marwick. I'd worked at Peat to earn my hours toward certification. I was hesitant to leave the prestige of Lincoln Center, but I wanted to be out of that misogynistic environment. There were a lot of unpleasant doings involving the board of directors at the time. (At one point, I received a call from a reporter for *New York* magazine wanting the real scoop. I knew everything, but I didn't want to burn any bridges. They did the article, but without any information from me.)

Hadassah was a huge organization. When I stepped into the role of CFO, I saw my annual salary jump from $35,000 to $52,000. For Ronnie and me, the additional money made paying for Eric's private-school tuition at Collegiate School on West Seventy-seventh Street and summer camp easier. It also afforded us the luxury of a Saturday-night babysitter. Joining Hadassah was like entering a wonderland. It was an environment strictly for women. I could wear pink suits, and family responsibilities were sacrosanct.

At Hadassah, I could leave at a reasonable time to pick up Eric at after-school activities. I no longer had to make excuses for personal emergencies. It was a wonderful position, and it met so many of my needs. Hadassah was a Jewish women's organization that firmly supported Israel. It encouraged me to be a wife, a mother, and a consummate professional. I was in the middle of union negotiations for the first time when I got a call from Eric's school; he had a fever and was being sent home. Our president, Ruth P., immediately directed me to be with my son. She arranged to have a car pick me up and had sandwiches made for us to eat when I got home. That night, she phoned to find out if Eric was feeling better. It was the perfect balance of work and family.

Shortly after I joined the organization, I made my first trip to Israel and reaffirmed my Jewish roots. Hadassah was a very large employer in the Land of Milk and Honey, with connections all over the country. I was meeting ministers, cabinet members, ambassadors, and people at the highest levels of society. It was then that I first started to gain self-confidence. My managerial and problem-solving abilities first surfaced, and I began to shine—it was empowering.

Bernie's secretary, Eleanor S., was leaving as I arrived on the eighteenth floor that afternoon. I knocked on his office door before stepping inside. I was secretly hoping to see that smile again, and I was not disappointed. Bernie was sitting behind his desk but quickly stood when he saw me enter.

"Please, come in." He walked across the room to greet me with a kiss on the cheek. Placing his hand lightly on my back, he led me to a pair of chairs. Bernie's office had a partial eastern exposure looking out toward the East River. Thanks to the building's curvaceous design, the office, like the others on the floor, was oval. The walls were transparent glass and provided an unobstructed view of the trading floor. There was no privacy. Eleanor's desk was just outside the door. It was strange being in a room where everyone could see what you were doing. I felt completely exposed. My office at Hadassah was twice the size of Bernie's, and when I wanted privacy, all I had to do was close the door.

The minute I sat down, a grotesque sculpture sitting on the credenza caught my attention. It looked like a giant screw. It was slate black and emanated an aura of meanness. It was probably famous and expensive, but it had a sinister quality, and it gave me the creeps.

After a few minutes of flirtatious chitchat, our conversation turned to business. This time Bernie explained how he would invest Hadassah's funds. At last I was able to grasp the theory behind his plan. There was a basket of approximately twenty blue-chip stocks; at the same time, puts and calls of the S&P 100 were purchased that acted as a "collar," or "hedge," against upside and downside risk. The basic strategy was that although you would never hit a home run, you wouldn't strike out either—the hedge limited any major gain and prevented any significant loss. It sounded great; it was just the type of thing Hadassah was looking for: consistency with minimal volatility.

At one point, I needed to use the restroom. Bernie showed me to his private bathroom.

"Only Madoffs can use this one," he explained. It felt like he was giving me exclusive permission to share his family's inner sanctum. I thought it was a slightly pompous thing to say, but I ignored it.

The bathroom looked like Batman's cave. The walls were

dark, and the fixtures were black. I found the way the soap scum showed on the sink after I washed my hands off-putting. I made a mental note never to use black fixtures in a bathroom.

When I returned, we resumed our conversation. Once again, our banter was effortless. Being with Bernie felt more like spending time with an old friend than with a business contact. He was kind, but at the same time there was a toughness about him I found extremely exciting. It was easy to see that his middle-class upbringing hadn't been polished away by the luxurious trappings of success. He had the rough-diamond persona down pat; he was down-to-earth but not without pretense. He would always let you know what he had, but also where he came from. It was a trait I found charming. There was a momentary silence when I mentioned that our broker at Prudential Bache had never heard of him. He had found no listing for Bernard L. Madoff Investment Securities in the financial directory. I wondered why.

"I'll send you something," he said, and smiled.

I was enjoying our talk and was disappointed when he told me we wouldn't be able to have drinks afterward. "My wife told me we have dinner plans," he said. "I'm so sorry."

What he meant to say was that his wife kept his social calendar.

"It's no problem," I said. The afternoon had validated the natural chemistry that existed between us. I had no illusions about anything becoming more personal. The thought had crossed my mind that he could be a good mentor, a friend who could aid and abet my career. Drinks or no drinks, I knew I would see him again.

"Well, thank you, Bernie," I said, reaching for my coat. "I think I have a decent understanding of your investment strategy."

"I wonder if there's anything else I can teach you?" The tone in his voice made it clear he was no longer talking investments. I hadn't missed the subtle way he'd touched my hand several times during our discussion. I couldn't tell whether he was only flirting or had more serious intentions. I must admit I was flattered. There was no mistaking his sexual innuendos. I didn't know how to respond to his overtures.

Fortunately, before I could reply, he apologized again about canceling. "I'm leaving as well. Come with me and I'll have my driver drop you off on my way home. You'll have a hard time getting a cab this time of day."

Bernie and Ruth lived about ten blocks from the office in a tan-brick high-rise on Sixty-fourth Street and Lexington Avenue. My apartment was another twenty blocks uptown. Ronnie and I were renting a two-bedroom in a doorman building at Eighty-second Street and York Avenue.

"It's been good to see you, Sheryl." Bernie waved as I stepped out onto the sidewalk. "I'll see you soon."

"I'd like that," I said. I was feeling giddy and grinning like a schoolgirl when I entered my apartment. I could hear the television in the living room as I fumbled with my keys. Before I could even take off my coat, Ronnie was there in the foyer. From the scowl on his face, it was clear that he was irritated. "Sheryl, you know you left your cereal dish in the sink this morning."

I could feel my insides tightening as I struggled for an appropriate response. Although we'd been married for years, Ronnie's angry tone could still twist me in knots. "You're right, Ronnie," I replied, trying to defuse his annoyance.

"Why can't you put it in the dishwasher right away?"

I wanted to just push past him, get into my nightgown, and go lie down. But he was hovering over me in his bullying, threatening way. I never knew what would set him off, but as I got older I did know that my mode of operation was to not push the buttons. Defending myself would be pushing a button. Ronnie was just looking to pick a fight, usually over something small and insignificant. It could be as minor an infraction as a hair in the bathtub or Eric using too much hair mousse or someone leaving a light on. He was intolerant of other people's frailties, but he would always have an excuse for his own. I had been living most of my adult live choosing not to verbalize my frustration because his overreactions would always end up being my fault.

Ronnie came from a place where he always looked to find fault. I came from a childhood where I was too ready to accept responsibility. We'd been in and out of marriage counseling, but Ronnie's erratic behavior was never clinically diagnosed. Whenever I described an explosive episode, he would blame me for creating the scenario that had caused him to lash out. In essence, he was making me the catalyst. Yet I was always fearful, afraid of what could be coming at me next.

Chapter Four

It seemed like Bernie's strategy was simple. He would buy stocks . . . reap the dividends from them in addition and hedge it by . . . buying puts and selling calls and I guess he would make some small returns. [The return] I was getting was not exorbitant. I mean, of course, looking back now, you know, how [he kept] such steady returns over all of these years . . . should have drawn more red flags but, you know, at the time, they certainly looked legit to me when I was trading there.

—former Madoff trader Adam Cohen, speaking to CNBC in 2009

About a week after my meeting with Bernie I received a letter from him at my office. It was a Xerox copy of his page in the financial directory. There was a paragraph with his various credentials at the top on page 1012, and a full-page ad for his brokerage firm on page 1013. On the bottom right-hand corner of the Xerox, Bernie had scrawled a message:

> *Dear Sheryl, your friend at Bache should have looked*
> *in the proper directory.*
>   *Love,*
>   *Bernie*

It was a slightly dismissive note, but the familiar way he signed it surprised me. It turned out that our guy at Bache worked in the retail brokerage business. He dealt primarily with individual trades, whereas Bernie was involved in the wholesale end. This explained why there was no listing for him in the directory the broker had checked.

Later that week, I went into a meeting with Ruth P. and our treasurer, Debbie K. They were thrilled that Bernie was willing to invest some of Hadassah's money. Like our French donor, Albert I., Bernie had several stipulations. He would invest Hadassah's money but would be unavailable to answer questions from anyone on our finance advisory board. When I asked him why, he told me the investment advisory side of his company was very small and he implied that he was doing this as an accommodation and didn't want to be bothered by people asking him a lot of questions. I wasn't overly concerned because the amount of money we were giving him represented a very small part of our overall portfolio. We decided to invest a few million dollars and see how it went. We all felt confident. After all, a donor with a good reputation had referred us to Bernie, and Bernie had been in business since 1960.

In late March, monies were wired to the Bernard L. Madoff Investment Securities account. Bernie later called to say that the funds had been received and invested. "I'm out of town, but I'll be back in two or three weeks," he said before hanging up. "Can I put you on the calendar for lunch?"

Bernie and I started making lunch a regular thing. He'd call my office every week or two, depending on whether he was in or out of the country. "The investments are going according to plan," he'd say each time I picked up the line.

"Bernie," I'd say, chuckling, "you know I don't even ask you about that."

His calls became so frequent that I finally asked him to stop having his secretary place them. There had been a few times when my secretary, Gladys F., had buzzed my office to say she was transferring a call from Bernie. I'd pick up and say something familiar only to find his secretary, Eleanor, on the line. I felt that we'd moved past the stage of a formal business relationship and requested that he call me directly.

Bernie liked to talk on the phone. The length of our conversations depended upon whether or not he was available for lunch that week. If we wouldn't be seeing each other, we'd spend a few minutes chatting and basically catching up. Bernie was always busy with meetings, and he seemed to travel constantly with his wife, Ruth. His life sounded rich and full.

Over the years, I started to see a pattern, and after a while, I figured out when and where he was traveling. Every few weeks, he and Ruth would go to a conference or an out-of-town meeting. They'd tack on a few vacation days at the end. They traveled first-class, visited exotic locales, and stayed at five-star hotels; it was a lifestyle I could only fantasize about.

Still, we continued to get together for lunch, and I looked forward to our time together. It always generated an element of excitement and gave me that familiar rush.

I don't think Bernie wanted me showing up at the office regularly because Ruth was there all the time. Her father had been an accountant, and she had worked in his office for years. Ruth was a graduate of Queens College. I was unsure of her role at her husband's firm, but I assumed it had something to do with accounting. To avoid any appearance of impropriety, Bernie and I started eating together at restaurants. Bernie would take care of the logistics. He'd choose the restaurant and make the reservations, and all I had to do was show up. As I was managing everything at work and at home, this was one less thing I had to arrange. I loved it.

We'd usually dine in Midtown at upscale places: Michael's, Bice, Aquavit, the Oak Room at the Plaza, the Mondrian, Essex House, and Lespinasse in the St. Regis Hotel (one of the five-star restaurants in the city).

At certain times of the year, we'd avoid Midtown around Bergdorf Goodman because Ruth would be out shopping in the area for the holidays. With Ruth on top of everything, Bernie was worried enough about how it might look if she saw us dining together. It was not a stereotypical "Hadassah lady," but an attractive forty-something who was out with her husband.

Ruth had Bernie on a short leash. He seemed genuinely afraid of what her reaction might be to seeing the two of us together. This seemed odd to me at the time. After all, we were only having lunch. None of the other male business associates I was meeting with at the time ever verbalized this type of concern. Maybe he was afraid she could read his mind. He rarely went anywhere alone. She accompanied him to dinners and functions and on most business trips. I wondered if it was because they'd been together for years, or because he'd given her a tangible reason to keep him close.

Bernie always arrived at the restaurant ahead of me to scope out a perfect table with a suitable seat. He was like Ruth P.: having his back to the room unsettled him. He needed to see who was coming in and who was going out. Once, the maître d' placed us at a table that had Bernie sitting with his back to the restaurant. He kept looking around, his eyes darting from the mirror on the wall behind me. He was either a social butterfly or he was looking for potential clients. He hated not being able to see what was going on behind him. His inability to focus on our conversation was so distracting I finally insisted we change seats.

If we ran into people we knew, we'd simply introduce each other; I was Sheryl Weinstein, CFO of Hadassah; he was Bernie Madoff, our investment adviser. It was a perfect cover. No one suspected our lunches were romantic interludes. His phone rang a lot during lunch. It was usually Eleanor. I assumed she knew when to call and when not to call. The constant interruptions prompted me to suggest that we start meeting for dinner instead. Bernie liked the idea, and soon we were getting together in the late afternoon for drinks and an early bite.

Bernie was a proud man, and right away I recognized his roots. He was self-made, and I admit that was something I found terribly attractive. He was impeccably dressed, and his clothes were precisely tailored. His shoes were highly polished, his shirts perfectly pressed. He wore Hermès ties and French silk knot cuff links. I had no idea that he collected cuff links. Whenever we were together he was wearing those same French silk knots. He felt the more elaborate gold and silver ones were not appropriate for the finance industry. He wore very little jewelry, just a plain gold wedding ring and an understated watch with a black leather band.

Bernie was like a multifaceted diamond, a man of many faces with a few discernible flaws. He possessed quite a few eccentricities. There had been a number of occasions when we were having lunch at a restaurant and he left a 10 percent tip or even less. I just thought it was an error on his part, that he was just careless. "I think you made a mistake," I pointed out. It was a habit of mine. I always double-checked Ronnie's addition because once in a while he would make a mistake. I am the ultimate caretaker and never wanted someone to be shortchanged.

Bernie appeared appreciative. "Oh, thank you."

On occasion, I corrected his "miscalculation" when figuring the taxi driver's tip. Despite his great wealth, Bernie used a paper clip to hold his money. He knew how to order exquisite wine, but he didn't drink.

"I don't drink at all," Bernie admitted during our first meal at a restaurant. "I tried it once and it didn't make me feel good."

He usually ordered a Diet Coke, Pellegrino water, or the occasional nonalcoholic beer. I never pressed him about it. I didn't feel it was my business to pry, although I was curious. He could have had an alcohol problem he didn't want to discuss. Perhaps this was a man who needed to stay in control. Looking back, I'm sure it had more to do with the many secrets he was harboring. He couldn't afford to let his guard down and say something he shouldn't. He had to be constantly on alert.

It took two or three months for me to realize that Bernie was primarily interested in talking about himself. He was a total narcissist, completely self-absorbed. He spoke about his travels, trips he was sponsoring, worldwide industry conferences, and the people he was meeting along the way. He was a bit of a name-dropper, but I didn't mind. They were interesting names, some of which I hadn't heard before. He spoke often of others in the investment world, such as Charles Schwab, head of the brokerage house that bears his name, Michael Bloomberg, and Arthur Levitt, then chairman of the Securities and Exchange Commission (SEC) and formerly a principal of Carter, Berlind, Weill & Levitt. I think it made him feel powerful having people competing for his financial services.

He bragged about the heavy hitters he knew on various charitable boards: Joanne Woodward of the New York City Ballet, and Howard Squadron, an influential and well-known attorney and philanthropist, and head of an important law firm in New York. He and Bernie were close friends. Squadron had introduced him to a number of powerful charitable organizations, and Sandy Gottesman, founder of First Manhattan, a New York money management firm, had asked him to become involved with Yeshiva University. Ultimately, Bernie served as treasurer of the board of trustees and board chairman of the university's Sy Syms School of Business until his indictment in December 2008.

Bernie disliked Donald Trump immensely. He referred to a time that Trump had had seats cordoned off for himself and his entourage at a movie theater in Florida. He thought Trump was a pompous ass. When the news quoted Trump saying Bernie had tried to get him to invest with him, I doubted it, but who really knows. Bernie's shtick was having people come to him. Why would he open himself up for rejection? He also wasn't too fond of former New York mayor Rudolph Giuliani. He told me he had been "harmful" to a number of his friends some years back when he was U.S. Attorney.

In 1990, when Bernie became the chairman of NASDAQ, he was far more impressed with his new title than I was. It was a title he held again in 1992 and 1993.

Bernie was not a religious man. To my knowledge, he and his wife did not belong to a synagogue. In fact, they often traveled to France on Yom Kippur, the holiest day of the Jewish calendar year. They would stay at the Plaza Athénée, a five-star hotel near the Champs-Élysées. I seem to remember Bernie talking about buying a flat in Paris, but when I later asked him about the apartment, he denied ever saying it.

Our conversations rarely centered on our spouses. Bernie never told me he was unhappily married. His wife was part of his life and his business, as were his sons. He indicated that at times he could be brazen and abrupt with Ruth. He admitted that on occasion he could even bring her to tears.

"I'm not known for my sensitivity," he remarked. Bernie said his wife was intimidated in the social circles in which they were traveling. She lacked confidence and could be self-conscious in the cliquey Upper East Side mentality of the wealthy or around very attractive women.

Bernie recounted a time when they were traveling and were taking a ride in a rickshaw. Minutes into the ride, the idea of being pulled by another human being disturbed Ruth so much that she burst into tears and insisted they stop the ride. She next directed her husband to pay the man the full fare. Bernie was annoyed that he not only paid the full fare but had to pay an additional large tip. While the story was meant to relate a sensitive side to Ruth, it revealed as much about Bernie. He viewed it as paying a lot of money for nothing. I understood where Ruth was coming from, but I also found that he brought the story around from being about Ruth to being about his own annoyance or generosity.

Bernie went on to tell me how many of his clients viewed Ruth as a daughter. There were also a number of clients who thought of Bernie like a son. He was very pleased about these close relationships he had with his clients. It appeared that he enjoyed the fact that these influential people held him near and dear. In contrast, he rarely spoke about his parents or his childhood. At the time, I found it puzzling.

In the summer and fall, there were long weekends in Montauk reserved for entertaining guests. They were called "friends," but they were always clients. How do you become sons and daughters of people if you don't take them into your home?

At lunch one afternoon I introduced Bernie to the economist Henry Kaufman. It's my understanding that

Henry later remet Bernie through his connections at the Palm Beach Country Club.

Bernie's self-aggrandizing behavior never bothered me. I think he was trying to impress me and at the same time bolster his own ego. I was, however, not an insignificant person. I had a noteworthy position in the world of philanthropy. At that time, Hadassah had a budget in the hundreds of millions. They owned and operated hospitals and schools in Israel. Next to the government, they were Israel's largest employer. They had their own building at 50 West Fifty-eighth Street.

Bernie was always telling me I had an interesting business life. "You see a lot of action during your day," he'd comment. I appreciated that he saw it that way. Bernie was also connected to many major donors. It was flattering that he liked me more than a little; it was also wonderful for my ego. There was no emotional pressure, no negative vibe. Even if our conversations were all about him, they were easy and relaxed. There were no arguments, no stress. He was never demanding.

With Ronnie, I couldn't talk fast enough. He had no patience to listen at all. If there was something bothering me, he'd say, "What do you want me to do?"

"You don't have to do anything," I'd tell him. "You just have to listen. I just want to share a thought with you without being attacked."

He'd get annoyed right away. "Get to the point. What's the point?"

There was little gray in our marriage; it was either black or white. There was always an undercurrent of tension. Bernie was pleasant and caring. He couldn't have been nicer or more gracious. He didn't have to lure me in. I thought we were kindred spirits. My personality blended very naturally with his—at least the one he showed me.

Chapter Five

By the time we'd been seeing each other six months, I'd picked up on a few of Bernie's eccentricities. In the middle of a conversation, he'd start blinking uncontrollably. He was constantly clearing his throat. Even when we spoke on the telephone, I would hear those clucking sounds. I assumed he was feeling more comfortable with me and therefore not trying so hard to control them, or perhaps it was quite the reverse. Maybe being around me made him more nervous. I remain convinced today that Bernie suffers from Tourette's syndrome* or some other

---

*According to the National Institute of Neurological Disorders and Stroke, Tourette's syndrome is a neurological disorder characterized by repetitive, involuntary movements and vocalizations called tics. The disorder is named for the pioneering French neurologist George Gilles de la Tourette, who first observed the condition in an elder French noblewoman in the late 1800s. Symptoms usually surface in children between the ages of seven and ten, can heighten in the teen years, and level off or lessen in adulthood. Males are three to four times more

undiagnosed neurological illness like obsessive-compulsive disorder.

Bernie rarely showed emotion. I can remember only one time when he expressed concern. He'd just been told that his grandson was exhibiting characteristics of obsessive-compulsive disorder. The boy was still very young, but Bernie felt responsible, and worried that perhaps he'd passed down the gene. Bernie confessed that as a child he used to line up his socks in the drawer. When he and Ruth were newlyweds and they were moving, he found the disorder and chaos so unsettling that he napped while his friends moved them. Disruption and disorder were the enemies.

Bernie liked sharing these flaws with me. I think it was his way of feeling connected. It didn't put me off: I was flattered that he wanted to let me in. Bernie was extremely superstitious. He would never read his fortune cookie when we dined at Shun Lee Palace, the upscale Chinese restaurant in the East Fifties. He feared it might bring him bad luck.

---

likely to be affected. Tics can be either simple or complex. Some of the more common include eye blinking and other facial irregularities such as grimacing. Simple vocal tics can include throat clearing and blurting out inappropriate things. Excitement and anxiety can worsen tics, as can certain physical experiences such as a tight shirt collar. While the cause of Tourette's is unknown, many people who suffer with the disorder can experience other neurobehavioral problems such as inattention, hyperactivity and impulsivity, attention-deficit hyperactivity disorder, and obsessive-compulsive symptoms such as intrusive thoughts and repetitive behaviors like hand washing as a result of neurotic worries about dirt and germs. Concerns about bad things happening can be associated with this ritualistic behavior.

Another of his obsessive tendencies centered on his wardrobe. Bernie loved clothes. "I have twenty-five suits of each color, and they're numbered," he admitted. He had custom-tailored suits from Kilgour on Savile Row in London; twenty-five blue and twenty-five gray lined up like soldiers in his closet on Sixty-fourth Street. They were identical and numbered so that he could match the slacks to the jackets. I found that very peculiar.

He once told me that his elder son, Mark, was "obsessive" about his clothing. My own son, Eric, witnessed this several years later. He had been hired to do an internship at the brokerage firm during his summer break from college. Mark nearly bit my son's head off after he and Eric accidentally bumped into each other and some coffee spilled on him. In spite of Eric's apologies, Mark Madoff stormed off in a huff.

When Bernie described his sons, they sounded spoiled and obnoxious. He was forever complaining about their lavish spending habits. Unlike their father, who'd grown up in a modest Queens neighborhood, Bernie's two boys had been raised in an upscale suburb on Long Island's North Shore. Roslyn was a wealthy, predominantly Jewish area, home to doctors, lawyers, and Wall Street bankers. It annoyed Bernie that Mark and Andrew insisted on flying every time they wanted to go to the family's waterfront home on Long Island's East End. Montauk was a two-and-a-half-hour drive from Manhattan—three in summer traffic. But the boys didn't care to spend their precious time in the car.

Bernie seemed amused by his son Mark's ongoing fear of kidnappers. Apparently Mark believed the Madoff fortune made him a target and he worried about his safety and his children's.

Summer was nearly over when Bernie invited me to lunch at the Four Seasons. As usual, he arrived before I did and got a prime table in the Grill Room. I was nervous, and the butterflies in my stomach made me queasy. My outfit was perfect. I made a habit of looking my best when I saw Bernie, and this day was no exception. I was wearing a black-and-white polka-dot suit with a peplum top, and Bernie greeted me warmly with the smile I'd grown fond of.

As soon as he saw me, Bernie rose from the table, took my hands, and kissed my cheek. Taking a step back, he looked up and down the length of my body. "Sheryl, do you know how incredibly sexy you are?"

Rather than speak right away, I smiled. *How am I supposed to answer a question like that?* I thought. Really, how can a woman answer a question like that? Bernie seemed enchanted by my sexuality.

When we were seated, the waiter came to our table with a glass of wine for me and a Diet Coke for Bernie. As I sipped my wine, I inhaled the ambiance of the restaurant. It had lofty two-storied windows and wood-paneled walls. This was the place where the "power lunch" had been born, and was a favorite of John F. Kennedy Jr.'s and Jackie O's. The Upper East Side social register considered the Four Seasons home, but the Grill Room was business-only territory.

After we'd ordered our meal, Bernie moved closer to me. "Sheryl, you know I think you're beautiful," he began, his eyes fixed on the table, not on me. "You're also an accomplished businesswoman. That's a knockout combination."

I smiled and thanked him. I told Bernie that my husband and I were going down to Atlantic City for a business conference. "I don't really like Atlantic City, and I don't like to gamble," I admitted. "Do you like to gamble?"

"No, I don't gamble," he said. "I don't want to look like the rest of the schmucks sitting there at the tables." Suddenly he leaned in toward me as if he was going to share a secret. "How about the two of us going off together somewhere?"

Had I taken a sip of wine, I would have spit it out. Reflexively, I leaned back. *Is this step number two?* I wondered. Obviously, he thought I was expecting a proposition and didn't want to disappoint me. Honestly, I never expected him to cross that line. I was totally taken aback. To quote an old expression, you could have knocked me over with a feather. The flirtation Bernie and I shared was simply that; nothing more, nothing less. I wasn't the type who could drop everything for a sexual romp.

I enjoyed our mutual attraction, and the idea of an affair had briefly crossed my mind, but the thought of taking our friendship beyond flirtation frightened me. And even if my husband was impossible at times, I still felt a sense of loyalty to him. I knew there was a big difference between enjoying Bernie's company and taking that next step.

Finally, I looked at him and started laughing. "I don't think so. Adultery is not my thing. It's not what I'm about. I've only been with two men in my life, my husband and my college boyfriend. I don't know what you must be thinking of me, Bernie."

"Well, that takes the pressure off," he said, sitting back in his chair. He looked enormously relieved. Suddenly he wanted to know all about me, when I met my husband, my entire life history. He was surprised that my life experience was so limited. I was part of the sixties generation, and he just assumed that I'd led a freer, fuller life. I'd lived through the sixties, but I didn't subscribe to free love, although sometimes I'm sorry I didn't. I still had one foot stuck in the fifties and wasn't ready to pull it out. It wasn't that I was a prude. Many of my friends had multiple partners. I, however, went from one long relationship to the next. And I was monogamous.

Our entrées arrived and we quickly changed the subject. In the years following our provocative conversation, I've replayed Bernie's comment in my mind dozens of times. For years I didn't understand exactly what he meant when he said "that takes the pressure off." But now I believe he felt relieved of any sexual expectations—he didn't have to be the aggressor. We could relax and be ourselves.

Chapter Six

For the next several years, Bernie and I carried on our "intimate" friendship. We'd get together for lunch when he was in town and stay in touch by phone when he was traveling. He'd take my calls even if Ruth was in the room. Once, I reached him at the office when he and Ruth were spending time with their grandson. Bernie seemed to enjoy his grandchildren. Most Wednesdays he and Ruth would drive up to Connecticut to see his grandson. Word was they were controlling. From our very first lunch, I understood that Bernie was very wrapped up with his family. I later heard stories to back up that impression. One of the issues at the core of his son Mark's divorce was the fact that Bernie and Ruth were supposedly micromanaging every aspect of their son's life; being a member of the Madoff clan became unsupportable.

Our phone conversations rarely involved business. In some ways, rebuffing his advances had allowed us to get closer. "Meet me for a drink after work," he'd say. We talked freely about our lives, often sparing no detail. When we met, there was always that flirtation, that underlying sexual tension, and plenty of verbal foreplay.

"I'd love to take you upstairs right now and ravish you," he'd tease if we were meeting at a hotel bar or restaurant. I often had lunch with other men—brokers, traders, and lawyers. I was a woman in a man's world. But I was always the client.

Bernie was different. He was constantly making sexual innuendos. He was surrounded by savvy Upper East Side social climbers who worshiped power and money. And here I was, a hardworking woman with no hidden agenda. We shared middle-class, down-to-earth backgrounds that offered us the perfect connection. Born on April 29, 1938, Bernie Madoff spent his childhood in Laurelton, Queens, a neighborhood in one of New York City's boroughs. It was an insular community, a snug Jewish enclave. Bernie didn't often speak about his parents. I have no idea what his father did for a living, but I later learned from a *Fortune* magazine article that Ralph Madoff listed his occupation as "credit" on his marriage license. In the article, a high-school classmate of Bernie's recalled that Ralph was either a "stockbroker or customer's man." The article explained that a "customer's man" was the equivalent of a client or account representative. It also reported that Ralph Madoff, who another of Bernie's friends claimed "looked like a truck driver," later went on to work for his son's brokerage firm. Bernie's father, one friend told the magazine, was "a rough-and-tumble kind of guy—not the kind of guy you screw with."

Ralph Madoff, according to *Fortune*, had once fought with the U.S. government over an unpaid tax debt. The senior Madoff, along with three others, owed $13,245.28 (a sum equivalent to $100,000 in today's dollars), which "caused the IRS to place a lien on the Madoff home." The article stated that the taxes were assessed in 1956, but the lien was not paid until after the house was sold in 1965, "suggesting that Ralph was either fighting the tax bill or unable to pay it." What I found most interesting was that according to the SEC, there was a brokerage firm with a Laurelton address registered to Bernie's mother, Sylvia, during the 1960s. The firm, Gibraltar Securities, was one of a number of companies under investigation for allegedly "failing to file financial reports." When Sylvia Madoff withdrew the registration, the agency dropped her firm from its inquiry. It is unclear whether his mother was involved in the securities industry or whether Ralph Madoff had filed the company in her name because of his tax troubles. Though the *Fortune* article claimed that Ralph Madoff worked for his son's brokerage firm for a time, I cannot confirm that, as I do not have intimate knowledge of Ralph Madoff's employment history.

Bernie claimed he was of Romanian and English descent. Supposedly, his mother's family hailed from England, but I never quite believed him. It seemed more likely that they had immigrated from Eastern Europe. I think one of the reasons he didn't speak much about his childhood was that it was not in sync with the image he was portraying in his adult life. I did wonder about that at the time. The little I did learn about his childhood revealed that Bernie's grandparents ran a bathhouse in Brooklyn, and Bernie and his siblings often stayed with them. Bernie loved the water, and swam in the pool after hours. He told me his grandfather had a *"lukshen"* strap that frightened him. *Lukshen* is the Yiddish word for spaghetti, and from Bernie's description, it sounded like the strap had strands of leather. It scared him to death. Over the years, Bernie expressed a macabre desire to be punished. He preferred "painful" deep-tissue massages to relaxing Swedish ones and made references to sadomasochistic sex, something we never explored in our relationship.

Bernie was the middle child. He didn't appear to be terribly fond of his older sister, Sondra. When he spoke of her, it didn't sound as if they were particularly close. Bernie was seven years older than his brother, Peter. He always spoke of him with great affection. Peter was chief compliance officer and senior managing director of Bernie's brokerage firm when Bernie and I first met.

Bernie loved to tell stories of how he initially funded his brokerage firm with the $5,000 he saved from lifeguarding and installing sprinkler systems. According to published reports, his business began to grow with the assistance of his father-in-law, accountant Saul Alpern, who allegedly referred friends and family members to Bernie. To compete with firms that were members of the

New York Stock Exchange and could trade on the Exchange floor, Bernie's firm started using pioneering computer information technology to disseminate quotes. That technology later became NASDAQ.

Bernie relied heavily on his brother because Peter was the "techie." He had a law degree from New York's Fordham University School of Law, and he joined the firm upon his graduation in 1970. Peter oversaw much of the firm's computerization.

Bernie's parents were both dead by the time we met. Bernie led me to believe that his mother had suffered from asthma and had died from some form of respiratory trouble. "It really wasn't a great way to go," Bernie reflected.

Bernie dated Ruth while attending Far Rockaway High School. Upon graduating in 1956, he left New York for the University of Alabama. He lasted one year. The following fall, he returned to New York. News accounts have stated that Bernie's decision to transfer to Hofstra University (then Hofstra College) in Hempstead, Long Island, a fifteen-minute ride from my childhood home, was so that he could be closer to Ruth. He received his bachelor's degree in political science in 1960, and went on to Brooklyn Law School. He attended classes in the morning and installed and repaired sprinkler systems in the afternoon. He never completed law school, dropping out after his first year.

Bernie's grandmother didn't like Ruth initially. She thought she was a "shiksa," the Yiddish word for a gentile woman, because Ruth was blond and had blue eyes. Of course, her family was Jewish. Nor were Ruth's parents terribly fond of their son-in-law when he and Ruth first married. Ruth's father was an accountant who earned a comfortable living, and Ruth's mother wanted a professional man for her daughter. "He won't amount to anything," they said. As newlyweds, he and Ruth accompanied his parents on their yearly jaunts to the Catskills. They had a relative who owned a hotel there, and it was a family tradition to spend the summer in the "mountains." Ruth didn't enjoy the trips, and she put a stop to them shortly after she and Bernie were married in 1959.

In the fall of 1990, I lost my father. It was very hard. He was in tremendous pain and decided to have a hip replacement. He consequently developed a blood clot and fell into a coma and died six weeks later. He was sixty-six years old. Bernie extended his condolences and told me he would provide a shoulder to cry on. He always struck me as the type of person who couldn't cope with emotional crises, and I doubted the sincerity of his offer.

I was very close to my dad growing up. He was the son of immigrants, a big man who stood well over six feet. He loved the opera and taught me to play chess at a very young age. My father was a gunner and a radio operator in the Air Force during World War II when he was eighteen years old. He received numerous Air Medals and was awarded the Distinguished Flying Cross. He suffered what is now called post-traumatic stress disorder. We didn't know that he had been sent "away" when he returned home from the service. It was something he chose not to share, for whatever reason. In fact, we didn't learn of it until after his death.

After the war, my father refused to fly again. He felt he'd had all the good luck anyone could ask for during his thirty terrifying missions over Germany and other parts of Europe.

His behavior could be inappropriate at times. He constantly hugged and touched me and played with my hair. My mantra as a child was "Leave me alone." He thought it was funny.

I had troubled parents and a troubled childhood, too. I was born January 19, 1949, at Brooklyn Jewish Hospital. I was an only child. My family lived in Brooklyn in a four-family house on East Ninety-third Street and Kings Highway. My grandparents, Fradel and Sam, owned their own four-family home on East Ninety-fifth Street. My grandfather owned a soda- and seltzer-bottling company. When they married, my parents, Murray Wasserman and Edith Katzman, were very young, and totally mismatched. A friend introduced them.

It wasn't an easy marriage. My parents were not blue-collar, but they were people of simple needs. My mother was a bookkeeper; my father was a marker and grader in New York's famed garment industry and was active in the union. He didn't make a lot of money. He worked six days a week and stood on his feet all day long. My father could be explosive. I remember violent fights between my parents when I was very young. The arguments grew less frequent as I got older. My father rarely got angry with me. But that all changed when I began to date. He was obviously not happy that I was growing up.

My mother's older sister, Ida, and her husband, Marvin, lived downstairs with my baby cousin, Robbie, and I spent most of my afternoons at their apartment. Aunt Ida didn't work and was always home. When I was seven years old, my mother went back to work. She took a job as a book-keeper at Prudential Financial in Manhattan, which later became Prudential Bache, to save up so we could buy a small house in North Massapequa. It was a typical Italian middle-class neighborhood on Long Island's South Shore. My grandparents helped out with the down payment.

Aunt Ida and Uncle Marvin were moving with us and had bought the house next door. Their house was ready first. After they moved, there was no longer an adult to supervise me during the long afternoons in Brooklyn. I was too young to be left alone, and I immediately got into mischief. My mother would leave the house early and I would get ready to leave for school on my own. That's when the trouble began. I started cutting school, and I discovered matches. We had boxes of big wooden ones, and I ran around Brooklyn throwing matches into piles of leaves. I found the smell of burning leaves intoxicating. One afternoon, I threw a lit match into the broom closet in the hallway. It wasn't exactly a three-alarmer, just a little bit of smoke.

I set my biggest blaze that November. The mail was on

the table in the dining room. I collected the unopened envelopes and went into the bathroom. I put the paper in the toilet, set the paper on fire, and closed the seat. I sat on the floor watching the bright orange flames through the crack between the toilet and the seat. Suddenly, the seat caught on fire. The fire was contained, but it left plenty of damage. I didn't know that my mother's Christmas club check was in one of the envelopes I'd torched. I found that out later.

After that episode, I never played with fire again. I did other bad things that year, though. I stole a ton of accessories for my Revlon doll from Ike's Toyland. For years, I worried that Ike was going to find out about my kleptomania and show up at our house. Every time a car came down the block, I was sure it was Ike. Somehow, I never got caught. More important, my mother never noticed all the stolen goods I'd collected. That was the extent of my life of crime.

I celebrated my ninth birthday in our new house on Long Island. My room was complete with cross-ventilation. My parents were not tidy people. They were heavy smokers and the ashtrays were always overflowing. The house was messy. My parents didn't like a lot of lights on, and they didn't like to keep the blinds open because sunlight would fade the furniture. Our house was usually on the dark side.

I spent every afternoon next door with Aunt Ida. The door to her house was always open. She and my mother were two sisters who never fought. Even Dad and Uncle

Marvin got along well. My aunt taught me basic household tasks. She was good at knitting and loved working with her hands.

My mother, on the other hand, was not a homemaker in any sense of the word.

I always had a feeling my mother had attention deficit disorder; she just couldn't sit still. She was constantly puffing on cigarettes and sipping on coffee. Plus, Mom always misplaced her keys and glasses. She was a social person, and people were naturally drawn to her. She could go into a diner and by the end of the meal everyone in the restaurant had become her friend. My mother was twenty-one when I was born, and for years people would mistake us for sisters. When I went out on a date, she would inspect me with a critical eye. She was concerned about my appearance, but she wasn't physically affectionate; no kisses and hugs from Mom.

I was molested when I was ten years old. One weekend, my parents were going out for the evening with Aunt Ida and Uncle Marvin. I was too young to stay alone, so my parents dropped me off for a sleepover at my father's sister's house in Old Bethpage. I liked Aunt Laura and her husband, Nat, although we didn't see them often. They lived in a cozy six-room ranch in a neighboring town and had two young sons.

After dinner we sat in the den to watch television. I was on the couch next to Uncle Nat when Aunt Laura disappeared into the kitchen to wash the dishes. Suddenly, Uncle Nat pulled me toward him, took my hand, stuck it in his crotch, and shoved his tongue in my mouth. I struggled to pull away, and I didn't tell anyone in my family about the "incident." But needless to say, afterward I found every excuse to avoid those "overnights."

When something like that happens, you feel ashamed and question what role you may have played. Was it something I provoked? Eventually, when I was much older, I told my mother about it. She told me everybody in the family knew of Uncle Nat's inappropriate behavior. Most of them had been targets, including Mom herself. I'm sure she thought I would be safe with Aunt Laura in the house.

I had an insular life until I went away to college. I wasn't exposed to the world at large. My parents didn't go into the city, they didn't go to the theater. They led fairly quiet lives. We ate out all the time, but it wasn't until I went away to college that I learned about prime rib and "medium rare."

My parents loved my husband, Ronnie. He'd grown up in Roslyn, where Bernie and Ruth had raised their sons. Ronnie's father was vice president of a commercial laundry business with headquarters in the Bronx. He was always happy when he was drinking, and he drank a lot. Ronnie's mother is still a beautiful woman. Our relationship was not easy at first, but over the years, we learned to love and respect each other.

When I met Ronnie, he was working in marketing for a children's apparel manufacturer in New York City. He soon left and went to work at the linen-supply company his father worked for in the Bronx. He had been there about nine months when he was offered a promotion. The company was not happy with their general manager in the D.C. plant and they offered Ronnie the position. Ronnie was excited, and he asked me to move to Washington with him.

"Let's get married," he said.

He gave me the engagement ring on Christmas Eve 1971, asking, "Are you sure you want to do this?" We had been living together in D.C. for a few months.

"Sure," I replied. He'd asked his parents for his Bar Mitzvah money to buy me a ring. They told him they'd spent it on his education, but would pay for the ring. They asked me what type of stone I would like. I told them an oval diamond. But when I opened the blue velvet box, I found myself staring at a pear-shaped stone.

Ronnie and I were married on Kentucky Derby Saturday. My parents threw us a beautiful wedding at the Woodbury Country Club on Long Island's North Shore. I had shopped for my wedding dress with my mother-in-law. My mother was working, plus she wasn't really a shopper and didn't feel in competition with my mother-in-law. I bought the second dress I tried on. It had a high collar, full sleeves, and a sweeping train that was removable for dancing.

We had almost two hundred guests, a great band, and great food. Ronnie and I danced to "We've Only Just Begun," by the Carpenters. Then we went out to the parking lot with our friends, got stoned, and came back inside to dance to our *real* wedding song, "I Want to Take You Higher," sung by Ike and Tina Turner.

We didn't go away for a honeymoon. Ronnie was serving in the U.S. Army Reserves, and he didn't want to be separated from his unit for the required two-week summer training session. We spent a few days at the Regency, an elegant hotel on Sixty-first Street and Park Avenue. There was a trade show at the convention center on Fifty-ninth Street and Columbus Circle that Ronnie wanted to attend while we were New York. We had friends up to the suite and called in for a pizza from Ray's on Third Avenue and Seventy-seventh Street.

I can only imagine what they thought of us down at the front desk. Here we were in a posh hotel with a pizza deliveryman in a sauce-stained apron heading upstairs to our suite. We spent three days in Manhattan before returning to D.C. The next weekend, Ronnie was on his way to Camp Drum in Watertown, New York, for his two-week stint. I planned to meet him the following weekend for a kind of second "honeymoon." He and his friends were staying at a motel outside of Watertown. When I arrived, Ronnie informed me of a development. He'd promised an army buddy he would share a room with him for the two weeks, and assumed that I would just be joining them in their room. That did not happen. I told him to get us our own room and give his friend the money for his share of theirs.

From the time we got married, every Friday night

Ronnie would bring me home a new negligee. Sometimes we spent half of the evening trying to figure out how it actually went on. It was so adorable the way he brought home these "gifts" for me. They were usually either red or black acetate. We didn't graduate to silk until many years later.

I was miserable living in Washington. Back in 1971, it was a quiet, conservative town. There was no activity in the evening, and I really missed the nightlife of New York City. When we first arrived, we took an apartment in Arlington, Virginia, about a half-mile from the Pentagon. After a year we moved to Rockville, Maryland, and eventually made some friends there. Ronnie was unhappy in his new job. He was not emotionally or professionally prepared for a managerial position. I was a city girl stuck in the suburbs with a husband who was under enormous stress and petrified of failure. I took a job at ITT Technical Institute, selling technical courses, and I began to thrive in the position. Soon I was earning more money than Ronnie, which made him feel even more insecure.

"I'm going to make more than you," he threatened, though I never viewed it as a threat. I thought that was fine and dandy. I had no problem with him earning more than me, and in fact didn't understand how that was a threat to me.

Ronnie made life difficult because of the discrepancy in our pay. He also hated that I was working evenings and weekends. He pressured me into leaving, and I went back to school. I took my first accounting course at the University of Maryland, and began working as a bookkeeper at a child-care facility on the campus of Prince George's Community College. Eventually, Ronnie settled into his position and began to excel. I still felt very lonely and missed my family and friends in New York. I was about six months pregnant with Eric when Ronnie was offered a job with partnership potential in Newburgh, New York. We picked up and moved to a garden apartment in nearby Spring Valley, a suburb thirty miles north of New York City.

I was happy to be back at home in the bosom of my family, but Ronnie was exhibiting the usual signs of stress in his new position. He'd been at the job about six months when he started having trouble with the owner of the company. I was in the living room caring for the baby when he arrived home one afternoon with his golf clubs and a carton containing the contents of his desk.

"I quit," he announced.

I was speechless. I wasn't concerned about his finding a new job. But who leaves a job without lining up another, particularly when they have a wife and a three-month-old infant at home? The next week, he was offered a job in Philadelphia. I was floored because he'd promised me that we were staying in New York. "I don't want to go," I told him.

"I'm going," he said. "You don't have to."

I reminded him, "You promised me we'd stay in New York."

"So I lied," he snapped.

Ronnie had been a poor student and grew up fearing

he would ultimately be a failure. He was a short, fat little boy, always getting into trouble at school. His father told him he was going to end up a truck driver or a ditch digger. He worked hard not to make that a self-fulfilling prophecy.

Pennsylvania was our third move in twelve months. Ronnie's irritability and frequent mood swings convinced me to return to school soon after Eric was born. I had been surprised by how much I enjoyed the accounting course at the University of Maryland. I wanted to have a profession so I could support myself and my child. I was tired of moving and being subjected to my husband's whims.

That January, I began taking classes at the Wharton School of the University of Pennsylvania. It was hard juggling my courses and the demands of motherhood.

For Ronnie, any stress would trigger anger; if a customer was unhappy, if he lost an order. Basically, I wanted to keep him as stress free as possible. I then had to complete two years of auditing in order to get my certification. I made a plan that would land us back in New York. We rented a one-bedroom apartment on East Eighty-second Street and Eric and I lived there while Ronnie stayed in Philadelphia. Not long after, I was hospitalized with a serious case of pelvic inflammatory disease and was in and out of the hospital for nearly two months. I had an abscess the size of a tennis ball. Eventually, I needed surgery.

Ronnie was commuting back and forth to New York on weekends to be with Eric. Eric was in nursery school and being cared for in the afternoons by a housekeeper I'd hired in preparation for my return to work. It was an extraordinarily stressful time.

I was one of the first women hired by Peat Marwick after the class-action suit filed against them in the 1970s. Getting the job wasn't easy. I didn't know about the interview process. I sent out my résumé to several firms. I had a 4.0 in my classes, but I didn't get any invitations to interviews.

It made no sense. I called Peat Marwick and said, "I have a 4.0, but I'm not getting any interviews. What's going on?" A recruiter called me back and invited me in for an interview. I didn't understand that potential job candidates were initially interviewed at colleges and universities. The firms had recruiters who scoured the nation's top schools in search of potential candidates. They didn't look at unsolicited résumés. Mine had been sent directly to the firm.

It was a two-step interview process. Initially, I met with the personnel manager in the audit division. One week later, I was invited to lunch with a senior member of the department at a nice Midtown restaurant. I had scheduled the interview between my intravenous antibiotic treatments at the hospital. Obviously, I didn't want a potential future employer to know about my health issue. Two weeks later, I received an offer of employment in the mail. The starting salary was $16,000. I was ecstatic. Peat Marwick was one of the Big Eight. It was the Ivy League of auditing firms.

I was one of the only women in my position who was married and had a small child. Men and women who were twenty-one and twenty-two years old surrounded me at the firm. Ronnie eventually left his job to start his own business in New York and we had someone come in the afternoons to take care of Eric. I had to get into the office by 8:45 A.M. and stay until 5:30 P.M., with forty-five minutes for lunch. The firm wanted you to bill a minimum of forty hours a week. I was just glad that I was able to get a start in my career. While I was there, I began specializing in audits of not-for-profit organizations, which led me to the job at Lincoln Center.

I had been at Lincoln Center only a short time when Eric started having pain in his joints. We had woods behind us in Woodstock, where we owned a small weekend house. He had "bull's-eye" rashes and was running fevers. It was very frightening. Nobody knew what it was, but they knew there were some children in the New York area who were showing these symptoms. Some were getting better and some weren't.

Luckily, our pediatrician put Eric on an antibiotic. The poor little guy could barely walk. It took a few months for him to get back to normal. They didn't know what the problem was back then. Only years later did we find out it had been Lyme disease from the bite of a tick.

I grabbed onto something back then. Anytime I was upset, I would say, "Eric is okay." That became my mantra. It was my bottom line. No matter what happened, it was all unimportant as long as Eric was okay.

None of the therapists I'd seen over the years had ever been able to explain my behavior to me. Then I read a book called *Women Who Love Too Much*, by Robin Norwood, and I realized it described me to a tee. I was someone who was always trying to change myself in order to please others. Reading the book helped me to understand that there was actually an explanation for what I was experiencing. At the time I read that book, I had been married for years. Working as a CPA seemed to validate my worth. That feeling contradicted the way I felt about myself at home. The disparity prompted me to read other books about verbally abusive relationships. Suddenly I was gaining perspective about my dysfunctional marriage.

Chapter Seven

It was the fall of 1992 when I traveled to Paris for the very first time, on business for Hadassah. Over the years, Ronnie and I had enjoyed trips to Italy, England, the Caribbean, and Florida, but we'd never been to France. We lived in Manhattan and enjoyed a home in the country like many of our Upper East Side neighbors. Our first weekend house was a "handyman special" in Woodstock, New York. We paid $35,000 for it in 1981. It had horrible green carpet with cigarette burns and mysterious stains, but we loved it. Five years later, we sold the place and bought a town house in a wooded area of northwest Connecticut.

The community was called Lakeridge. It was a 235-acre gated community near the picturesque town of Litchfield. Ronnie and I spent every weekend there for many years, barbecuing and socializing with friends. We were a group of about thirty couples who enjoyed hanging around together swimming and playing tennis. We were in our late thirties and forties, and most of us worked in Manhattan. This was our weekend home. We had mopeds and often took scooter rides around the community. In the evenings, we hosted and went to great parties.

I started traveling for work when I joined Hadassah. In the beginning, I was away about three times a year for a week to ten days at a time. I'd make at least one trip to Israel to work on one of our projects, and I'd attend the midwinter conference at the Concord Hotel in Monticello, New York. There was also the national convention, which took place in any number of cities in the United States. I was interacting with interesting people; dignitaries, politicians, and doctors and professors at the hospital in Jerusalem.

At first, I really didn't enjoy traveling. Eric was still very young, and I'd get extremely nervous before a trip. I hated flying. I felt I was losing control. I usually relaxed and settled down once I was in the limo on my way to the airport. As Eric got older, my anxiety over being away from him lessened.

The prospect of traveling to Paris on my own was thrilling. I had arranged to meet with our mysterious donor, Albert I., in the French capital, and then continue on to Jerusalem. Our then treasurer, Marlene P., was already in the City of Lights. She'd accompanied her husband there for a medical conference. Marlene had never met Albert, and was eager for an introduction.

I had met Albert briefly during a prior visit to Jerusalem in 1990. It was by coincidence that we were both in

Israel at that time. I was there on Hadassah business and Albert was in town visiting with relatives. When I learned that he was planning to have lunch with two of our doctors at Hadassah Hospital, I asked if I could join them.

Of course, I was immensely curious about Albert. After all, he'd been the one who'd introduced Hadassah—and me—to Bernie Madoff. In fact, it was one of our doctors, Henri A., who'd first introduced Albert to Hadassah. They'd met at a Spinoza symposium, and after listening to Henri speak, Albert expressed interest in his cutting-edge research in the area of human biology. Albert's donation was made specifically to fund Henri's human biology research facility at Jerusalem's Hadassah Hospital.

Albert was in his late seventies, sophisticated, understated, and gracious. He looked like a kindly, white-haired professor. Our lunch in the cafeteria was pleasant and brief. During the meal, I learned that there were complications with the facility he was so generously endowing, and after speaking with several staff members at the hospital I realized that Albert had not been receiving the treatment I felt a donor of his level was entitled to. There appeared to be difficulty in getting the project off the ground, with the Israelis questioning aspects of the building plans for the research facility he was funding.

I remained disappointed with the way the hospital staff was treating Albert, and was determined to meet with him in Paris to express Hadassah's appreciation in a more professional manner. I consulted with Bernie about proper etiquette when contacting Albert. Bernie had shared with me that Albert was a bit reclusive, and I was uncertain if he would be open to a visit. Bernie offered to reach out to him on my behalf.

I knew that Bernie traveled to France with some regularity to see Albert. I was under the impression that Albert was one of Bernie's major clients. After all, Bernie had told me how close the two men were. Albert viewed him like a son, he claimed. It was what he said about so many of his clients. Over the years, I'd listened to Bernie describe the details of his Parisian jaunts. He and Ruth always stayed at grand hotels not far from the Champs-Élysées. The five-star Plaza Athénée, on the city's Right Bank, was their favorite. Bernie's list of places to see was in my purse when I set off for the airport. Clutching my passport, I hurried into the terminal at JFK International to catch my flight, which was scheduled to land in Paris early Friday morning. My meeting with Albert was set for that very evening. After a snafu with my luggage, I was in a cab and en route to the hotel. Marlene and I were staying at the InterContinental Paris–Le Grand in the Ninth Arrondissement, near the Opera House. I arrived at the hotel in time to freshen up and rest for a few minutes before Dr. A. picked me up at the hotel and drove me to Albert's flat. His apartment was close to the Eiffel Tower. It was one of those grand old apartments with high ceilings and elaborate moldings. It was foggy that evening, and from the living-room window I had an unobstructed view of the base of the Eiffel Tower through the mist.

Albert greeted me warmly. We sat in the living room and enjoyed his wife, Doris's, homemade cookies. Doris was like a shadow; after a quick hello, she came into the room, left the cookies, and disappeared. I knew from Bernie that Albert's wife also was a recluse. She was an American, and had been living in Paris for years. She may have suffered from agoraphobia—she rarely left the apartment. Bernie called her "Miss Marple," the name of Agatha Christie's elderly spinster turned detective.

My time with Albert was delightful. It had been rumored that in his past he had been treasurer of a sub-rosa political party in France. He was born in Romania and had been living in Paris since before World War II. He'd traveled there to study and work as an engineer. When the war broke out, he attempted to return to Romania and was denied reentry because of his Jewish heritage. It was so traumatic that he told me he could no longer speak Romanian. He joined the Underground, and miraculously, he survived the war. He settled in France and went into the cement business. He realized that it was more lucrative to be the middleman rather than to take ownership of the cement, and apparently he made much of his fortune that way.

During our discussion, I promised Albert I would do what I could to ensure that the hospital project moved along expeditiously.

"Do you see Madoff?" he asked.

"We see each other occasionally," I replied.

"Bernie is lucky he gets to see you."

Albert briefly explained how he'd met Bernie. He spoke highly of him. "You can trust him," he assured me. "He's a good man."

Marlene arrived at the apartment near the end of Albert's and my meeting. Together, we presented him with two gifts, a Lucite statue and a *tsedakah* box (a charity box). He was like a delighted child.

That night, Henri A. met us at Albert's, and Marlene and I left with him for dinner at Les Deux Magots, the landmark French restaurant in Saint-Germain-des-Prés. The meal was fabulous. The following evening, Marlene's husband and another couple joined us for a night at the famed Moulin Rouge. I saw the Opera House, enjoyed a bus tour of the city, and visited the Galeries Lafayette, the largest department store in Paris.

It was a whirlwind weekend, and I was still reeling from the excitement of it when I boarded the plane for Israel that Sunday. Before me, I had a week of business meetings in Jerusalem.

Later on I learned that in addition to Albert's generous donation to Hadassah, he also set up a charitable foundation in Israel named for the seventeenth-century philosopher Yeshaya Horowitz.

The sun was rising over the East River when I arrived home from Jerusalem on a November morning. Our doorman waved me in. I left my luggage for the porter and walked to the elevator. I noticed the concierge picking up the phone the minute I passed his desk. I couldn't wait to get upstairs and jump in the shower. I was exhausted and grimy after the transatlantic flight. In 1989, Ronnie and I had bought the apartment, a wonderful two-bedroom on the sixteenth floor of a building on Seventy-second Street, off First Avenue. The apartment was everything I had wanted, or thought I would ever be able to have. That it wasn't on Park Avenue didn't matter.

Eric was thrilled about the move. We had more space, and a terrace with three exposures and room for a small table and chairs. When my father first came for a visit he remarked, "Oh, it's like a little ranch house." We had finished putting in a granite foyer and renovating the master bathroom, the first of many improvements we hoped to make. When the elevator door opened onto my floor, there was Ronnie standing in the hallway in his bathrobe.

I jumped. "Oh my God. You scared the crap out of me! What are you doing out here?"

"Everyone's okay," he reassured me. "But there's been a little accident."

Apparently, my husband had instructed the doorman to call upstairs the minute I arrived. He wanted to prepare me for what I was about to find when I entered our apartment. My heart sank as I braced myself for impending doom. The renovations had been completed before I left for Paris, and I had arranged to have the carpets professionally cleaned. Ronnie didn't want to be stuck in the apartment all day waiting for the crew, so he'd left our keys with the doorman. We had a halogen floor lamp in one corner of the bedroom. The men unfortunately moved it under the swag drapes while they worked. The heat from the lamp promptly set the drapes on fire. In a panic, the men fled the apartment, yelling, "Fire! Fire!" Someone heard them and dialed 911.

In their rush to evacuate, the men left the keys inside the apartment, and the door automatically locked behind them. By the time the fire department arrived and broke down the door, the flames had ripped through the entire bedroom. Everything was destroyed, right down to the concrete walls.

I couldn't believe Ronnie had left the carpet-cleaning crew alone in our apartment, but I didn't dare say it aloud. It would have triggered an avalanche of anger beyond belief.

Later that morning, as I sat in the middle of the devastation, my secretary, Gladys, phoned from the office.

"Bernie Madoff called and asked to hear from you," she said.

As I dialed his phone number, I feared I would burst into tears the minute I heard his voice. "Hi, Sheryl. Welcome home. How are you?"

"I'm sitting here in my bedroom," I replied, my voice breaking. "It burned down to the ground."

"I'll come and help you clean it up," he said. We talked for a few minutes as I delivered the details of my latest calamity. "Let me know what I can do to help," Bernie soothed. I couldn't help doubting his sincerity. I had a feeling altruism wasn't in his DNA. He quickly changed the subject.

"Listen, we're doing a trade with treasuries, and I thought of Hadassah." He wanted possession of the treasuries; he was going to use them to do a trade, to get a percentage point or two like you would on a bank account. "Do you have any that you can send over?"

This was the first and only time that Bernie asked for money. "Let me check our balances and I'll get back to you," I said.

His request was unusual, but why would I question his motives? It sounded to me like an opportunity to make a few extra dollars. I had been pleased as Hadassah's investments increased over the years, but I was uncomfortable with the fact that Bernie never wanted to speak with anyone on Hadassah's financial advisory board. His good friend Albert operated the same way. I sometimes wondered if Bernie's connection to Albert was designed in order to meet European investors. And at one point, Henri told me that Albert said he and Bernie were partners.

Bernie denied it. "That's not true," he said. "I don't have any partners."

"Oh, I just thought that somebody mentioned to me that the two of you were partners," I stammered, reluctant to betray any confidences. It never would have occurred to me that Bernie was trying to cover up the ultimate subterfuge, a gigantic Ponzi scheme.

I phoned Bernie back later that day. "We have some

funds available. I'll wire them over." Looking back, I realize that Bernie's offer to make us a part of his treasury deal had come at around the same time federal investigators began looking at whether Bernie was connected to a suspected Ponzi scheme in Florida.

Their inquiry centered on two accountants, named Frank Avellino and Michael Bienes, who had set up an unregistered hedge fund of nearly half a billion dollars and had been funneling investors' money to Bernie since the early 1960s. Within days of the SEC's inquiry, they agreed to return the money they'd raised and to pay a fine. Bernie was obviously trying to cover a half-billion-dollar shortfall.

The New York Times later reported that archived documents from the 1992 case revealed "numerous red flags that raise questions about the SEC's failure to examine . . . Mr. Madoff long before Mr. Madoff's Ponzi scheme spread worldwide." Bernie's name did not appear in the agency's complaint, which referred only to an "unnamed broker."

I didn't know anything about it. But later that month, someone from Hadassah's financial advisory board sent over an article from *The Wall Street Journal*. I felt my stomach churning as I read the headline. Bernie's firm was part of an overall investigation that involved a possible Ponzi scheme. "Oh my God, the organization is going to lose its money," I muttered. "I'm going to lose my job."

I'd always felt there was something behind those beautiful eyes. From the beginning, Bernie had asked that we not reveal that he was taking care of Hadassah's money. He indicated that he didn't want to speak to members of the organization's finance advisory board. Its members included some of the top financial people in the nation. That had been his initial caveat upon agreeing to take on Hadassah as an investor. At the time, he'd made it seem as though he didn't want to be bothered with questions; he was investing Hadassah's money more as a favor. He also didn't want others coming to him with requests to be included in the fund. Bernie was always very adverse to publicity. *Still*, I wondered, *why all the secrecy?*

His desire to be under the radar made me uneasy, but it wasn't a red flag. I felt a lot of people in his position were like that. "Who was the broker with the Midas touch?" the article asked. "The mystery broker turns out to be none other than Bernard L. Madoff—a highly successful and controversial figure on Wall Street."

I was enormously relieved as I reached the end of the article. While the story had begun with a potential link to a possible Ponzi scheme, the allegations against Bernie appeared to have been baseless. According to *The Wall Street Journal*, the SEC had done a thorough investigation, and Bernie had been exonerated. Here were two reputable names, the SEC and *The Wall Street Journal*, reporting that Bernie Madoff was cleared of any wrongdoing. The SEC stated that all the monies were accounted for; everything was fine. There it was, in print. There was no subterfuge—Bernie Madoff had been cleared.

"Mr. Madoff is one of the masters of the off-exchange 'third market' and the bane of the New York Stock Exchange," the article read. "He has built a highly profitable

THE WALL STREET JOURNAL

MONEY & INVESTING

Wall Street Mystery Features a Big Board Rival

Bernard L. Madoff

But the mystery broker turns out to be none other than Bernard L. Madoff — a highly successful and controversial figure on Wall Street, but until now not known as an ace money manager.

Mr. Madoff is one of the masters of the off-exchange "third market" and the bane of the New York Stock Exchange. He

Regulators feared it all might be just a huge scam. "We went into this thinking it could be a major catastrophe," says Richard Walker, the SEC's New York regional administrator.

But when a court-appointed trustee went in, the money *was* all there. Indeed,

This article, which appeared in *The Wall Street Journal* in December 1992, exonerating Madoff of suspected fraud and proclaiming him "an ace money manager," finally convinced me that it was safe to invest my life savings with him.

securities firm, Bernard L. Madoff Investment Securities, which siphons a huge volume of stock trades away from the Big Board. The $740 million average daily volume of trades executed electronically by the Madoff firm off the exchange equals 9 percent of the New York Exchange's."

Bernie claimed that he didn't know the money he was managing had been "raised illegally" and insisted the returns were really "nothing special," given that the Standard & Poor's fifty-stock index generated an average annual return of 16.3 percent between November 1982 and November 1992. "I would be surprised if anybody thought that matching the S&P over ten years was anything outstanding," he told the *Journal*.

The only thing that surprised me was the number of Bernie's investors. He'd always bragged about having a small coterie of investors. Now I was beginning to see that he was operating on a much broader scale.

After the story about Bernie's Ponzi scheme broke in December 2008, thousands wondered why the SEC hadn't smelled a rat. Both the SEC and the NASD regularly audit firms, and they ask numerous questions during their audits. If they couldn't find frauds as world-shaking as Madoff's, how will this failure impact investors' views of the financial industry?

Part Two

Chapter Eight

By the fall of 1992, life at home with Ronnie was becoming more of a challenge. Eric was seventeen years old and starting to assert his independence. His quest for autonomy was creating an explosive dynamic between him and his father. Their arguments would become so heated, I'd hear them the minute I stepped off the elevator. I could feel my stomach tightening as I followed the shouting down the hallway to our apartment. To spare Eric, I became the buffer. My putting myself in the middle drove Ronnie crazy.

In the past, when I had thought about leaving Ronnie, the idea of being alone seemed far worse than enduring my turbulent marriage. I remembered what a friend once told me. She was a divorced single mother and knew about my issues with Ronnie. She said, "As bad as it gets, it's still better than being alone." And until now, I had believed her. But with my budding self-confidence and Eric leaving for college, there were fewer tangible reasons to stay.

Still, the concept of being alone was frightening to me. As I began to picture a life without Ronnie, a new thought entered my mind. Having a boyfriend might help ease the transition from married to single. Up to this point, having a physical relationship with Bernie Madoff had never been an option. I was under no illusion that an affair with Bernie would blossom into anything permanent. He was far too wrapped up in his family to engage in anything more than a temporary tryst. That was just fine with me.

During the past five years, our friendship had become special. Bernie seemed grateful that I didn't take him too seriously. His travel schedule was grueling, and like anyone in a position of power, he had a coterie of people vying for his attention. Someone always wanted something from him. When we were together, the pressure, as he'd said, was off. Sometimes he shared his frustrations about his sons if they were being too loose with his money or about people in the industry who were driving him crazy. I was someone he could talk to on a deeply personal level with the confidence that I would never reveal what was said. Our friendship allowed him to vent, and he afforded me the same luxury. However, I never had this need to share with him what was going on at home because I didn't want to blow my image, considering he thought I was this very independent, confident, successful woman. I thought he might view me differently if he learned about my relationship with Ronnie. I thought he would not have viewed me with the same admiration and unavailability if he knew that I felt browbeaten in my other life. Of course, as with all relationships, there are always three sides. Hers, his, and reality. I didn't want to disclose that side of me. Still, the chemistry between Bernie and me was palpable.

About four months after the article appeared in *The Wall Street Journal,* I started talking to Bernie about personally investing with him. He'd been earning consistent returns of between 18 and 20 percent for Hadassah since 1988; nice, steady returns. The financial advisory board found nothing unusual because treasuries were also having returns in the teens. The SEC investigation had revealed that everything was kosher with Bernie's firm. This was the reassurance I needed to trust him with my money.

In March 1993, Bernie and I were having drinks at the St. Regis Hotel when I bit the bullet and asked him if he'd be willing to handle my personal funds. "It's not much," I said. "We only started saving money when I joined Hadassah. I'm afraid what we have will be well below your minimum."

He reached across the table and stroked my hand. "It's my company, Sheryl. I make the rules. And for you, I'd be willing to make an exception."

"I'm very nervous about it, Bernie," I confessed. "I'm anxious about giving that kind of control to anybody." Financial security meant everything to me. I needed to be 100 percent sure that Bernie was on the up-and-up before I gave him a dime.

Bernie made it sound so logical. "I understand," he

said. "But if I need help, I delegate. I give jobs to those who are best equipped to carry them out. If I'm looking to decorate, then I hire a decorator. If you want your money invested, you go to the best investment broker available," he reasoned.

Then it hit me. I realized I had to have a comfort level of trust in this area before I could take our relationship further. Little did I know Ronnie's and my hard-earned $70,000 would be contributing to the Ponzi potpourri.

After that fateful dinner, Bernie and I caught a cab outside the restaurant. I took his hand. Though we'd touched before—a kiss on the cheek, his hand over mine at the table—this was different, and I felt a buzz of excitement. I don't remember what we were talking about, but as I turned to face Bernie, there was something new between us.

Bernie leaned toward me and stroked the line of my jaw. I stopped speaking and brushed his lips with mine. His hand pulled my face closer, and I felt his tongue gently touch my lips. He tasted of the dessert we'd just shared, sweet and delicious. I don't know how long we kissed, but all too soon the cab pulled up in front of my building. When I pulled away, my heart was racing, and though I'd had only one glass of wine, I felt tipsy.

"Well," I said.

"Well, indeed." In the darkened cab I could still see his beautiful smile. "It's about time."

I had to laugh. "Good night, Bernie. See you soon."

"You can count on it." He pulled me in once more for a soft, gentle kiss. "Good night, Sheryl."

I was still smiling when I walked into my building.

Once I felt I could trust Bernie with our personal funds, everything else was easy. Ronnie and I worked hard for our money. It validated me and allowed me some degree of safety and security. Being able to trust Bernie financially allowed me to trust him in a more intimate way.

It was a little scary at first, but once I made the commitment and the statements started coming, I felt a sense of relief: investment decisions for my mother and for Ronnie and me were now in the hands of Bernie Madoff. Before turning over my life savings to Bernie, I'd discussed it with both of them. Even though I was a finance professional, investing was not my forte: oversight and management were my strong points. Still, Mom was all for it.

"If it's a great investment, then why not?" she said.

Mom was going to transfer her money, too. She had hers with a broker at New York's David Lerner Associates. She had IRAs and bank CDs, and as they came due, I liquidated them and transferred the funds over to Bernie.

It was July when I first started receiving my statements, and they made me smile. It came as no surprise to me that I would have to enter the information manually each month. At Hadassah, I had a clerk who entered all the data when the statements arrived every thirty days. Other than the number of shares and the balances, my statements were identical to Hadassah's. They were three to four pages in length and printed on eight-by-fourteen gray-and-white paper. As with Hadassah's, I too had to enter all the transactions, the buys and sells, to calculate the gains and losses on each security. It could take any-where from fifteen minutes to forty minutes, depending on how many trades there were. It was not only a matter of entering the numbers but making them balance as well.

It was not something that was typically done on a retail brokerage account. Bernie said these accounts were being handled like wholesale brokerage accounts, and that's why they didn't provide any type of service. The state-

DATE	BOUGHT RECEIVED	SOLD DELIVERED	TRN	DESCRIPTION	PRICE OR SYMBOL	AMOUNT DEBITED TO YOUR ACCOUNT	AMOUNT CREDITED TO YOUR ACCOUNT
				BALANCE FORWARD			15,945.46
12/10				CHEVRON CORP	DIV		324.80
				DIV 11/15/07 12/10/07			
12/10				UNITED TECHNOLOGIES CORP	DIV		83.20
				DIV 11/16/07 12/10/07			
12/11				JOHNSON & JOHNSON	DIV		307.10
				DIV 11/27/07 12/11/07			
12/13				MICROSOFT CORP	DIV		220.80
				DIV 11/15/07 12/13/07			
12/17				COCA COLA CO	DIV		170.00
				DIV 12/01/07 12/15/07			
12/17				WACHOVIA CORP NEW	DIV		307.20
				DIV 11/30/07 12/17/07			
12/21		1,760	2215	PFIZER INC	23.040		40,460.40
12/21		660	3559	AMERICAN INTL GROUP INC	55.900		36,860.00
12/21		800	6508	PROCTER & GAMBLE CO	73.300		58,608.00
12/21		230	7808	BOEING CO	87.310		17,454.00
12/21		330	10861	SCHLUMBERGER LTD	91.270		29,194.40
12/21		1,140	12085	BANK OF AMERICA	42		47,855.00
12/21		1,560	15094	AT&T INC	40.920		63,773.20
12/21		1,240	16378	CITI GROUP INC	31.250		38,701.00
12/21		260	19359	UNITED PARCEL SVC INC CLASS B	72.250		16,775.00
12/21		420	20671	CONOCOPHILIPS	83.280		34,961.60
				CONTINUED ON PAGE 2			

DATE	BOUGHT RECEIVED	SOLD DELIVERED	TRN	DESCRIPTION	PRICE OR SYMBOL	AMOUNT DEBITED TO YOUR ACCOUNT	AMOUNT CREDITED TO YOUR ACCOUNT
	1,450,000			U S TREASURY BILL DUE 04/03/2008 4/03/2008	99.149		
				MARKET VALUE OF SECURITIES LONG 1,445,135.30 SHORT			

One of my account statement from Madoff Investment Securities shows the growth of my savings. The steady returns made the thought of moving my money elsewhere seem irrational.

ments didn't show the gains or losses, just the purchases and the sales of the security.

I think a lot of women look to their husbands to take care of them. In my marriage, I had been taking care of our finances, but now I was relieved of that responsibility. My "boyfriend" was taking care of me. That didn't mean that I wasn't reviewing the statements. I had a whole financial advisory board, some of the top people in the field, reviewing Hadassah's statements. We'd already had a five-year history with Bernie and he had done well for us. There were always questions being raised as to how he was achieving the incredible results. He obviously counted on the SEC's being complicit or negligent. He was using the agency's lack of findings as his smokescreen.

It's unbelievable how he was able to inspire this kind of confidence. The magic was in the returns. No one knew the formula. The moment I surrendered my funds, I got caught in Bernie's web. There was no exit strategy. Why in the world would anybody in their right mind transfer funds when money was being made? Where else would they put it that was not volatile? From our very first statement, we began to see our investment grow.

I was attending a meeting of Hadassah's finance advisory board in the spring of 1993 when some of the members asked for a meeting with Bernie. Because of his stellar performance, the organization's fund had done well in the four years Bernie's firm had been managing Hadassah's investment. The board was doing its due diligence by wanting to speak with Bernie about his approach. These were some of the top investment people in the city, the state, and the world volunteering their time to serve on behalf of Hadassah. I think part of what was prompting the board members to call a meeting was curiosity about the man. The 1992 article in *The Wall Street Journal* had already been published, indicating that Bernie was an "ace money manager." When I asked if he could meet with members of the board, Bernie didn't give me a hard time, and in fact agreed very easily. I thought it was most likely because he wanted to please me.

Ironically, I was on a bus heading down Fifth Avenue to Saks when I spotted Bernie's black car pulling up in front of Rockefeller Center. It was the first day of Passover, and the offices of Hadassah were closed. One of the members of the advisory board had an office in one of the buildings at Rockefeller Center, and the meeting was taking place there. I watched out the window as he stepped out onto the sidewalk and strode toward the entrance. Bernie looked very debonair in his suit and long khaki overcoat.

The meeting that day appeared to have gone well. Members said Bernie was doing a good job, although they admitted they weren't sure how he was doing it.

Not long after our first kiss, Bernie and I were having dinner at the Palace on Madison Avenue. He liked to eat at hotel restaurants because they were quiet, and the tables were farther apart. We'd just placed our order when he surprised me with an unexpected proposal. "Would you care to go upstairs? I've a room reserved for us . . . if you'd like."

My pulse quickened, and I felt my chest growing tight. "You're kidding, right?"

"No, I'm not kidding." He grinned. "I reserved a room for us." He leaned in closer to me, but we didn't kiss. He wouldn't have risked being seen by someone he knew. Still, I could feel his warm breath on my neck. "Do you want to know the room number?"

"I don't even know how you feel or smell," I stammered.

Bernie chuckled. Playfully, I pulled him toward me. "Come over here," I demanded. "Let me see what you smell like." Jokingly, I sniffed his collar, inhaling his musky European cologne. I think he sensed he was moving too fast. I'd only just raised the possibility of an affair and already he had a room reserved. I heard him whisper, "It's okay, Sheryl. I'm not going anywhere. You're worth the wait. Just don't make me wait too long."

When I got home that night, I was curious. Had he really reserved a room? I decided to place a call to the Palace to satisfy my curiosity. "How many floors do you have?" I asked when the hotel operator answered. Sure enough, Bernie had given me a valid room number. The executive suites were on the top floor.

A few weeks later we met in the Library, a bar at the Palace.

The weather that February day was unseasonably warm. The streets and sidewalks were crowded with people returning from work. I loved the sounds and smells of the city.

We didn't have much time. Bernie had another meeting that evening. We were walking toward the exit when somebody called his name. He stopped and I kept walking, pretending we weren't together. Outside, I waited for him, and we walked along the sidewalk together. Up ahead I saw a doorway that was set back from the sidewalk. Just as we were passing by, I grabbed the lapels of his jacket and pulled him inside. For a moment we were alone in the dark. Drawing him close, I kissed him. His lips were soft and accepting, and until then, I hadn't realized the intensity of desire that had been building inside me. I let my hands run through his silky gray hair and breathed in deeply, filling my senses with his presence. I felt his hands pulling my hips toward him. I wanted more.

Once I gave him the green light, our slow, seductive dance was in motion. One night over dinner, he surprised me when he announced, "I could really use a little S and M." I had no idea if he was serious. I simply ignored him. Another time, he invited me to join him at the Oak Room in the Plaza Hotel at Fifth Avenue and Central Park South. The décor was rich and masculine, with detailed wood-paneled walls and a barrel-vaulted ceiling. The lights were low, and candles burned on each table. There was an additional degree of privacy at the small, café-style tables tucked into the corners of the room.

Bernie and I preferred to sit catty-corner. We had been there only a couple of minutes when I started massaging his inner thigh beneath the crisp, white tablecloth. He didn't take my hand away; he just sat grinning. "I'm going to have to walk out of here backward," he joked.

Now that we had taken our "friendship" to the next level, we longed for the kind of intimacy new couples share. We wanted to sit close and hold hands over dinner, something not possible out in the open. While I had been the one to open the door, I was still an old-fashioned girl at heart. I wanted Bernie, but I was not yet ready to jump into bed with him.

"How about we have dinner in a hotel room?" Bernie asked.

"Sounds great," I said.

Our time together was titillating; we were both having a great deal of fun. It was strange territory for both of us, naughty and exciting. We loved it.

"Do you think you can really handle the passion?" I asked him over drinks.

Smiling, he assured me he could. "What am I going to do with you?" he announced playfully. "You're going to be a big problem for me." Little did he know how big a problem I would turn out to be sixteen years later.

Chapter Nine

We had our first official "date" at the Lowell, a boutique hotel on Sixty-third Street just off Madison Avenue. The quaint, redbrick structure rose seventeen stories and sat on a quiet, tree-lined street two blocks from the penthouse Bernie shared with his wife.

Until now, our relationship had consisted of stolen moments in restaurants and bars throughout the city. We decided a hotel room would offer us the privacy we craved. The Lowell was perfect. Bernie reserved a one-bedroom suite on the ninth floor. He phoned me a few hours before we were to meet to give me our room number. I took great care getting dressed. Beneath my suit was a sexy silk chemise I'd bought for the occasion.

I felt dizzy as I stepped out of the taxi onto the hotel's welcoming red carpet. I was extremely excited and nervous as I strode into the European-style lobby. Bernie was waiting for me, and we took the elevator up to the ninth floor together. "Sheryl, you know I love the way you look in that blouse," he grinned. Before he could even push the button, I grabbed his lapels and tried to kiss him.

"Not here," he warned. "There could be cameras."

The room had a prewar aura of formality with old-world furnishings and heavy drapes. There was a living area with two couches, a coffee table, a desk, and a working fireplace, and a beautiful bedroom with a king-size bed. The door had barely closed behind us when Bernie pulled me near and kissed me gently. "It feels nice to finally have you in my arms," he said softly.

Pulling me closer, he pressed his lips to mine. I had waited so long for this moment. As I kissed him, I noticed that he had lowered his eyes.

"Bernie, how come you're not looking at me?" I asked.

"I'm shy," he replied with a bashful grin. This wasn't our first kiss, so I was a little surprised by Bernie's sudden timidity.

After hanging our coats in the front closet, we moved to the couch. A quiver of excitement coursed through me as he took my arm and began to kiss the inside of my wrist. His lips slowly made their way to the nape of my neck. His touch was gentle and tender. Bernie and I had ordered up sandwiches. As he took my breath away, I heard a knock at the door. It was room service with our dinner. The Lowell has an excellent restaurant, the Post House, downstairs. Bernie taught me about Dijonaise sauce that night. I was sitting across the table when I noticed him mixing the mustard and mayonnaise together on his plate.

"What are you doing?" I asked.

That's when he told me about Dijonaise.

Our trysts were never about the meal. We ate because we hadn't had dinner. There was nothing rushed about Bernie. He wasn't a grabber. He didn't run around the room chasing me. It was like a dance, slow and sensual and appropriate. In that room we created our own world. In it, we were ageless.

After dinner, we returned to the couch for "dessert." Closing my eyes, I allowed myself to enjoy Bernie's soft kisses. He was a great kisser. I liked the way he followed my lead. Suddenly, I found myself in the role of the aggressor, feeling incredibly sensual and turned on by my reawakened sexuality. Our lips were locked as we crossed the floor to the bedroom, both of us giggling as we flopped onto the bed. Bernie was on top, kissing me, when suddenly I felt as though I were suffocating.

"You have to get off me," I puffed. "I can't breathe."

"Oh, sorry," he said, laughing as he rolled me over on top of him.

"You're one beautiful woman, Sheryl." I could feel his erection through his pants.

It was nearing nine o'clock when we called it a night. "Do you want me to leave first or do you want to leave first?" Bernie asked.

"You leave first," I said. I needed some time alone to get my thoughts together.

Once he left, I collapsed on the couch, poured myself another glass of wine, and replayed the evening's events in my mind. It was the first time I had been involved with somebody I didn't consider gorgeous. My relationship with Bernie broke the looks barrier. Being with him was not about sex; it was about making my first real adult connection. He wasn't my "type," but this time I wasn't choosing someone based on outward appearances.

By the end of the evening, I had terrible beard burn. I have very sensitive skin, and my face was red and blotchy when I left the hotel. I really wasn't worried about questions from Ronnie. He thought I was out at a business meeting. I had many meetings in the evenings with Hadassah, both finance meetings and meetings with donors. Besides, at that time Ronnie suffered with such rampant attention issues that he didn't seem to notice anything I was doing.

The next morning, I realized I'd left my sunglasses in the hotel room and called Bernie to find out how I could get them back.

"They'll be waiting for you at the desk," he assured me.

I took a cab to the office that day. It was convenient that Sixty-third Street ran west, and I instructed the driver to wait at the curb while I raced inside the hotel to retrieve my glasses. (The big, Jackie O–style sunglasses were back in fashion. When I went to kiss Bernie, it was like a collision. Bernie wore progressives. Initially, he had trouble with them. It seemed as if it had taken some time before he finally got them fitted properly.)

A few weeks later, Bernie and I returned to the Lowell.

Again, he called to let me know our room number. When I arrived he was already in the room. He had had his secretary, Eleanor, make the reservations in person to ensure that the room would not turn up on his credit card. I have no idea what Eleanor knew or what she believed Bernie was or wasn't doing at the hotel. He could have just been meeting a masseuse in the room. I'm sure it was something he was keeping from Ruth, but whether she suspected an affair I don't know. I assume he was smart enough not to say, "I'm meeting Sheryl Weinstein to get it on."

Although he trusted her discretion, I felt it was important enough to have Bernie call me directly so she didn't know how often we spoke, although she did make the restaurant reservations for us. She was always very friendly and engaging when we did speak on the phone.

Bernie was taking off his jacket when he pointed out the plane tickets in his inside breast pocket. "They just gave me these at the office to bring home. They're for my in-laws. I'm such a good son-in-law. My mother-in-law thought I'd never amount to anything," he said, waving the tickets in the air. "Boy, did I surprise her."

We were sitting across the table from each other when I walked over, straddled him, and opened two of the buttons on my blouse. He looked down and moaned.

"Have you had surgery?" he asked.

"No." I smiled. "I have my mother to thank for these. But you can check for scars if you want."

From my vantage point, his receding hairline was clearly visible. Bernie was nearly all gray, and his hair was starting to thin near the top. "Propecia?" I blurted out.

Bernie was not a girly man. His "How could you think that of me?" expression let me know he understood I was referring to the foam solution that is supposed to grow and retain hair. That look said it all.

My trysts with Bernie continued into the summer months. We'd spend long evenings kissing and cuddling. That's as far as it went. "I've been told I'm good at kissing and this type of stuff," Bernie joked. He was always kidding around with me. He didn't take himself too seriously. Although Bernie seemed to have been ready that night back at the Palace, I was still hesitant. I was enjoying our courtship and was perfectly content taking my time. In between our dinner "dates," we continued to meet for lunch whenever Bernie was in town. I wanted to assert my independence and occasionally picked up the tab for lunches and dinners. Bernie liked the idea of being treated. Over lunch one afternoon, he joked about how he'd failed the written portion of the Florida driving test a few times, until the woman at the motor vehicle bureau took pity on him and passed him.

It was spring of 1993 when Eric received an acceptance letter from Emory University in Atlanta, Georgia. He was excited as he prepared for his freshman year. He planned to spend the summer working as a counselor at Timberlake Camp in upstate New York. He was to leave for college a few days after his return.

I was looking forward to having him out of the house—no empty-nest syndrome for me. The stress at home was finally going to end. The night before we were to drop Eric off at camp, Ronnie and I were in the bedroom watching television. Ronnie was surfing the channels when he stopped on the news program 20/20. They were airing a special on adult ADHD* (attention-deficit hyperactivity disorder). The show highlighted the story of a couple and how the disorder had impacted their lives. At the end of the program, they provided a list of symptoms and mentioned a nonprofit organization called CHADD (Children and Adults with Attention Deficit/Hyperactivity Disorder). Looking over at Ronnie, I realized he had virtually all of the symptoms that had been described. I tried to speak with him about my suspicions, but I couldn't

---

*According to the National Institute of Neurological Disorders and Stroke, attention-deficit hyperactivity disorder (ADHD) is a neurobehavioral disorder. While symptoms may appear as innocent and merely annoying nuisances to observers, if left untreated, "the persistent and pervasive effects of ADHD symptoms can insidiously and severely interfere with one's ability to get the most out of education, fulfill one's potential in the workplace, establish and maintain interpersonal relationships, and maintain a generally positive sense of self," according to J. Russell Ramsey, author of *Cognitive Behavioral Therapy for Adults*. Adult ADHD patients complain of difficulty with concentration, attention, and short-term memory. The most common psychiatric conditions that may have overlapping symptoms with adult ADHD include mood disorders, anxiety disorders, substance-abuse disorders, antisocial personality disorder, borderline personality disorder, developmental disabilities, and certain medical conditions, according to *Psychiatry* magazine.

get him to engage in a dialogue. He wouldn't even look at me.

The following Monday, I got to the office early. I immediately called ABC, the network that had aired the program, to track down a number for CHADD. Someone at CHADD referred me to several psychiatrists in the New York area that dealt with ADHD in adults.

Later that week, I flew to California to attend a Hadassah convention. I gave Ronnie the names and numbers of the psychiatrists before I left for the airport. Handing him the list, I said, "Do what you want with these."

Ronnie was going to join me in Los Angeles the following week for a ten-day vacation. I was dreading his arrival. Vacationing with Ronnie could be terribly stressful. I never knew if he was going to be in a good mood or a bad one. I was surprised when he called me in California a few days later to say he'd seen a doctor, who had put him on a low dose of Ritalin.

"I don't feel a difference," he insisted.

Deep down I think Ronnie realized how much our marriage had deteriorated. His relationship with Eric was also suffering. They'd always had a wonderful bond, but it was going downhill fast. Was it possible to believe he could change?

Ronnie's next phone call informed me that contrary to Ronnie's strong admonitions, Eric had quit his job at camp and was returning home from upstate. He was eighteen, and missing his girlfriend in New York.

There goes my summer, I thought.

Once Eric was back in New York, Ronnie put him to work loading trucks at his place of business. Eric enjoyed the physical labor—he didn't feel as if he was being punished for quitting his camp job. He stepped up to the plate and became one of the guys. (When Ronnie and I returned from our vacation, I found Eric a clerical job at Hadassah, where he worked for the remainder of the summer.)

A few days later, Ronnie arrived in California to begin our vacation. I immediately noticed a difference in his behavior. The first thing I observed was the change in his driving style. He often yelled at motorists who got in his way. He could be very aggressive and get easily frustrated. But as I sat beside him, I marveled at his calm demeanor. However, when the Ritalin wore off, he went back to his usual irritable self. One day he begrudgingly acknowledged that the medication might be working. He'd taken a tennis lesson at the hotel. When he came back to the room that afternoon, he was beaming. It was the best lesson he'd ever had. For the first time, Ronnie had found the patience to listen to the instructor. He improved his game that day.

In late August, Ronnie and I flew to Atlanta to set Eric up in his dorm room. I felt relieved that the constant conflict would subside. On the flight home I gave Ronnie a book on ADHD. We had been in the air a few minutes when suddenly he started to cry. Reading about the characteristics of ADHD had dredged up painful memories of his childhood.

I had mixed feelings. Here was a man who, for years, had acted as if he could barely tolerate me. He had finally been clinically diagnosed. Ronnie had a "condition." I had to find a way to replace my negative feelings toward him with compassion and empathy.

But how?

Chapter Ten

By September, the sexual tension between Bernie and me had reached new heights. After months of intense kissing and fondling we still hadn't had sex, but we knew it was inevitable. We were about to explode.

Bernie had been ready to go from the moment I signaled that I might consider taking our relationship further. But I had been married a long time and felt conflicted about being unfaithful. Yet it was unlikely our relationship could continue like this.

In spite of Ronnie's diagnosis, I still couldn't put all those hurt feelings behind me. I had endured years of emotional and verbal abuse and was waiting for the next episode. I felt like my marriage was about over.

A coincidental trip to Washington, D.C., presented the perfect opportunity for me to spread my wings. I was working at my desk one afternoon in early September when Bernie called. We exchanged some pleasantries, then he announced, "I'm going to Washington next week for a securities industry meeting."

"Oh, really? I have a meeting there next week, too. What day will you be there?" I asked. My meeting was scheduled for the fourteenth.

"I could be there on Monday for my meeting on Tuesday morning," he answered.

"That's when I'll be there." I said.

"Well"—he paused to clear his throat—"do you think we should stay in the same hotel?"

"Absolutely."

"Okay. I'll take care of it."

Being away from our immediate surroundings would give us the freedom to think about taking the next step. The rest of the week passed quickly. I didn't see Bernie, but I spoke to him briefly about the hotel arrangements. We were staying at the Willard InterContinental Washington, where Bernie's meeting was being held. After catching the Delta shuttle from La Guardia, I arrived at the hotel early Monday evening. Steps from the White House, the hotel had hosted every U.S. president since the 1840s. Both the "Battle Hymn of the Republic" and Martin Luther King's "I Have a Dream" speech were written within its hallowed walls.

I felt nervous and excited as the taxi pulled up to the hotel. The building's limestone and terra-cotta façade, triangular shape, and beaux arts architecture conjured images of New York's Flatiron Building. Soaring columns and polished marble floors engulfed me the second I stepped through the revolving glass doors. The lobby was buzzing with excitement that day. The Oslo Accords between Palestine and Israel had been signed, and the public ceremony with Yasser Arafat and Yitzhak Rabin had taken place a few blocks away.

After checking in at the front desk, I looked for the elevator and went to my room. The accommodations at the Willard were lovely. Red velvet window drapes provided a dramatic backdrop for gold and cream upholstery and crisp white bed linens. There was a king-size bed and a desk, and two windows that faced into another wing of the hotel. It wasn't much, but I wasn't there for the view.

I wanted to freshen up a bit before my date with Bernie, but I didn't want to get my hair wet. I was blow-drying it straight back then. I decided to take a bath and relax. The anticipation I felt about the upcoming evening had grown each day since we made our plans. We hadn't specifically spoken of what the evening would entail, but it was obvious where we were headed. As I soaked in the tub, I considered how strange it would be to sleep with a man who hadn't initially appealed to me physically. There was a gentle shyness about Bernie that I found endearing. And probably most enchanting was the way he made me feel. With Bernie I always felt wanted, desired, and that was an empowering sensation. During the past few months, the thrill—the buzz—of sexual tension had only gotten stronger.

I had carefully planned out what I would wear that

evening, down to the negligee I'd purchased at Bloomingdale's especially for after dinner (I have never worn it again). I had intended to wear beige silk pants, a beige silk camisole, and a beige and black silk jacket. But the dry cleaner didn't have the camisole ready when I arrived to pick it up. At the last minute, I had to substitute a black silk camisole, which was a break from my typical monochromatic style. The sexy negligee was black and had deep slits on the sides. It tied together with silk ribbons. I thought Bernie would love it.

I had fleeting thoughts of Ronnie. I realized I felt guilty about sleeping with Bernie. But I already felt emotionally separated from Ronnie. He had berated me for years, and I still couldn't shake the hurt and anger. How lovely to have only good feelings. I had dressed and was applying a final touch of makeup when Bernie called my room to let me know he'd arrived. We agreed to meet downstairs for dinner. The thought crossed my mind that it would be a welcome relief not to be worrying about who might see us together.

For a big city, New York was an amazingly small town. It seemed to stretch from Fifty-seventh Street to Eighty-sixth Street, from Fifth Avenue down to First. Bernie and I were both easily recognized in the fishbowl that was the Upper East Side. This made it almost impossible to go anywhere without being seen. Being away from home allowed us to exhale and finally lock out the rest of the world. Before I left my room, I hung the negligee on the back of the bathroom door. I was nervous!

I was meeting Bernie in the the Willard Room in the lobby. It was a formal dining room worthy of a head of state. It surprised me that he'd chosen to dine at the hotel's restaurant. He was having a committee meeting at the hotel in the morning; surely some of those attending would be overnight guests. Bernie didn't appear concerned. He rose from the table when he saw me enter the dining room. "I've missed you, Sheryl," he said. As he leaned in to kiss me, I inhaled the faint scent of cologne.

Bernie and I sat close together, holding hands under the starched tablecloth. Bernie was dressed in his usual attire: navy blue suit, light blue shirt, and coordinating Hermès tie. He wore his French silk knot cuff links and plain gold wedding band. Bernie had nice hands. His skin was soft, and his nails were beautifully manicured.

We enjoyed a romantic candlelit dinner. At one point, I felt myself getting very warm; beads of sweat formed on my forehead and between my breasts. To cool myself down, I pressed a cold glass against my face and neck. Bernie didn't seem to notice; if he did, he didn't say a word.

We'd been in the restaurant almost two hours when the check arrived. I was nervously anticipating the rest of our evening, and I found myself on edge as we rode the elevator to the executive floor. Our rooms were around the corner from each other.

"I'd like to freshen up a bit," I told Bernie as we neared my door.

"That's fine." He smiled and disappeared down the hallway. It felt like no time had passed before I heard a knock at the front door. When I opened it, there was Bernie.

"Can I come in?" He stepped over the threshold. Once he was inside we talked for a while, and he took a look around the room. "Wait a minute. I'll be right back," he said. I had no idea where he was going when he left the room.

A moment later I heard knocking on the other side of the door inside my room. I opened it to find Bernie standing there, smiling. Apparently, he'd reserved adjoining rooms. He remarked on how much bigger his room was than mine. I didn't care. I wasn't going anywhere. This room was my safe zone. Here, I could be in control.

We kissed for a bit before I excused myself. It was time to bring out the negligee.

Bernie had stripped down to his silk boxers when I emerged from the bathroom. I found him perched on the edge of the bed. The delighted expression on his face said it all. "Sheryl, you're beautiful," he pronounced. I had never seen Bernie without his shirt. He had a nice build; he wasn't muscular, but he was toned. Bernie had been an avid skier and a competitive swimmer in his youth. His weight tended to fluctuate—all those charity dinners. He was forever watching his diet.

I felt sexy and empowered in my slinky nightgown. Sauntering over to Bernie, I perched on top of him. I was straddling his legs as I kissed his lips gently. It turned me on that he was secure enough to let a woman take the lead sexually. I assumed it was because he was a self-made man and felt secure in his own skin. From the beginning, he'd responded positively to my sexual dominance; we were always in perfect sync during our marathon kissing sessions. As I stroked his bare skin, Bernie suddenly flew into a full-body convulsion. He almost catapulted from the bed as though a tremor had ripped through him.

"Bernie, are you okay?" I asked. I was worried that he might be having a heart attack.

His eyes were blinking furiously. "Yes, I'm fine."

I didn't want to make a big deal of this peculiar episode. He soon settled down and acted as if nothing had happened. Clearly, my touch had unleashed some sort of involuntary response, a massive tic, a spasm of some sort. As soon as we resumed our lovemaking it happened again. His body jolted again. "Bernie, are you sure you're okay?" I asked.

"Yes, Sheryl, I'm fine."

We got back to business and took our time. Bernie was very sensual. I think it really turned him on when I got on top. I was turning myself on as well. Our lovemaking was slow and familiar. It seemed perfectly comfortable. There was none of the awkwardness that I had anticipated.

Before Bernie, I'd been with only two men. Still, I knew this man was not well-endowed. We had dimmed the lights in the room and I couldn't see his penis, but it didn't fill me. Much to my pleasant surprise, I was able to achieve an orgasm. Good sex was not lacking in my life, but this was. It was about releasing years of pent-up anger and frustration. It felt great to finally let some of it go.

Afterward, Bernie remained close and held me in his arms. "Are you one of those women who likes a man to stay with you?" he asked.

"No," I said with a laugh. Truthfully, I needed time to digest what had happened. It had been many years since I'd been with anybody other than Ronnie. I really had no idea how I was going to react.

Bernie put on his boxer shorts, and stood to gather his clothing. Pausing at the door, his suit neatly draped over his arm, he said, "I'd like to get you a little bauble."

"Bernie, I don't need a bauble." I was firm about this part of our relationship. I wasn't interested in Bernie's money. Of course, I was turned on by his power and financial success, but his money was not what our connection was about.

Flipping on the television, I caught a few minutes of Conan O' Brien's late-night premiere. "I never would have believed that I would have my own TV show any more than I would believe Rabin and Arafat would be shaking hands," the talk-show host joked.

The next day, Bernie and I went our own ways. I didn't see him again in D.C., and we flew back to New York on separate planes. When I saw Ronnie that night, I was smiling inside.

I was in the office when Bernie phoned me that Wednesday. "Did you get back all right?"

"Yes," I said. "How was your meeting?"

"Fine, fine." Rosh Hashanah, the Jewish New Year, was right around the corner.

There was a long pause. I heard the familiar clucking noise Bernie made when he was clearing his throat. "So, now you know about me," he blurted out. I nearly choked on my coffee. I knew exactly what he meant. Bernie had a very small penis. Not only was it on the short side, it was small in circumference. That he was now pointing it out to me was telling. It clearly caused him tremendous angst. I wanted to be careful how I responded. Men and their penises have a strange and unique relationship.

"I didn't seem to have a problem," I told him, pointing out that I'd achieved orgasm with no difficulty. I liked this man and didn't want to emasculate him. His tiny penis hadn't prevented me from climaxing.

The tone in his voice indicated that he was relieved. "I'm going away for a while," Bernie told me. He and Ruth were traveling with New York Mets owner Fred Wilpon and his wife, Judy, major contributors to many New York charitable organizations. "I'll call you when I get back."

According to Bernie, the couples were good friends. (Not surprising, the Madoffs were "friends" with all their clients.) Earlier Bernie had boasted that they'd invited him to travel with them to celebrate their thirty-fifth wedding anniversary. Bernie sounded very pleased about investing "the Mets' money."

When we hung up, the silliest thought crossed my mind—I remembered that expression "big swinging dicks" of Wall Street. I smiled to myself, wondering how many of those "big swinging dicks" out there are actually compensating for teeny-weeny ones.

I wondered if Bernie's need to get it out in the open between us stemmed from insecurity. At puberty, it's common for all of us to privately compare our bodies to our peers'. Boys in particular put great emphasis on the size of their equipment. It's common for them to talk about the size of their penises. The one with the smallest is often ridiculed. Studies have shown that male adults still feel inferior when their penis is small, and in some cases they believe they can't please their woman because they don't have bigger equipment. These negative beliefs and views can lead to a lack of self-confidence—which can be reflected in a man's everyday behavior. It can affect how he handles stress and his work performance. It can even lead to a mild case of depression created by the man's belief that others, especially his wife or girlfriend, view him as being not particularly well-endowed.

Studies have concluded that for a man, having a small penis is probably worse than being too short or going gray at an early age. A review conducted by Drs. Kevan Wylie and Ian Eardley of the Porterback Clinic and Royal Hallamshire Hospital in Sheffield and St. James' Hospital in Leeds, United Kingdom, concluded that "about 90 percent of women actually prefer a wide penis to a long one." The review, which is based on the combined results of more than fifty international research projects into penis size and small penis syndrome (SPS) conducted since 1942, also found that 85 percent of women reported being satisfied with their partner's penis size, compared to only 55 percent of men who were satisfied with their size.

Men with this "problem" can view every instance in which they have to "show off" what they have as a hardship. Changing in a locker room, going swimming, even making love can become something they fear rather than take pleasure in. They are afraid of the ridicule they may face when first having sexual relations with a woman.

Most of the time, it makes no difference to the woman. Even so, the man can still view it as a huge barrier. Body image impacts self-esteem. Self-esteem impacts personality, morality, and work ethic. What you feel about yourself determines how you interact with others. Many things affect self-esteem.

In the case of Bernie, he didn't strike me as a person who had issues with self-esteem. He was self-made. That usually takes care of self-esteem issues. True, he was consumed by himself. It had taken a few months for me to realize that most of our conversations centered on him. Still, that he felt compelled to mention it had me wondering. Perhaps he felt pressured, and this was his way of getting it out in the open.

Was Bernie really self-assured, or was he covering up for feelings of inadequacy?

Chapter Eleven

I shared my extramarital affair with a handful of close
friends. They knew I was unhappy and supported my
desire to explore a relationship outside my marriage. Bernie's constant blinking prompted me to give him the nick-
name "Winky Dink." This is how my friends and I referred
to him whenever we discussed the affair. He blinked all
the time when he was with me, and not so noticeably when
others were around.

"I want you to remind me that he is not going to leave
his wife," I told one girlfriend. My feelings for Bernie had
grown, and I didn't want to go there because it just wasn't
going to happen.

I thought about Bernie a great deal. I missed him, and
at times I found myself replaying moments of our night
together in D.C. I was very revved up and in control. I
had this very powerful special boyfriend. I was feeling
really good. With Ronnie now on medication for his ADHD,

he'd begun to notice aspects of my behavior that had eluded him in the past. One day, I was in the kitchen, lost in thought, when suddenly he asked, "Where are you?"

I have a very expressive face, and sometimes I'll have conversations with myself. I must have muttered something aloud that had sparked his interest. "Oh, no place," I replied and went to the refrigerator to get a soda.

Bernie would leave voice-mail messages for me on my new cell phone. "Hi, it's Bernie. I'm thinking about you. Looking forward to seeing you soon."

To me, sex with Bernie turned out to be surprisingly exciting. It was a time of exploration—of learning how to move in a way that was pleasing to both of us. Because he and I had spent so many evenings together at the Lowell, we had already tested the waters. Adding sex to the equation brought on a new level of intensity. Now when we met for lunch or dinner, something as simple as a kiss stolen in the doorway of Shun Lee Palace was a promise of things to come.

I felt so totally alive! It was a feeling that had been missing in my life for years. Instead of love and romance, there had been anger and fear. My affair with Bernie provided an outlet for the passion that had been dormant for so long. When we made love, I was on fire. Bernie was a release valve, someone I could disappear with for a few hours. Somebody who would say nice things to me and treat me like a lady. He was an older man, and he was chivalrous. He opened doors for me, stood when I entered restaurants, and was never short on compliments. Bernie was my oasis. I could be very feminine without giving up my self-respect. He was the first significant man in my life who didn't make me feel like things were my fault or that I was inadequate. This was fun.

That fall, Bernie and I met for "dinner" at the Palace. He'd sent his secretary, Eleanor, to make the reservations. (He told me Eleanor was beginning to feel uncomfortable. She told him that she hated showing up with no luggage and paying for the room in cash. She felt people were looking at her "funny.")

Bernie had reserved a small one-bedroom suite on the top floor of the hotel. It was an executive floor and accessed by a private elevator. Our room had a great view of the Midtown skyline. When I got there, the table was arranged with hors d'oeuvres, wine, and a fresh bouquet of flowers. Bernie liked to relax as soon as he arrived at the room. The minute he came through the door, he took off his shoes and plopped down on the couch. It was just the two of us, and he could finally unwind. It had been almost a month since our last sexual encounter, but we didn't jump right into bed. We spent the next hour eating and talking. On the way to the hotel, I had decided to stop at Bergdorf Goodman to give myself a little spritz of my perfume.

"You smell wonderful, Sheryl," Bernie commented. "But

we have to be careful. I don't want my clothes to smell of perfume." Bernie spoke a little about his family, and I told him Eric had gone off to college, and about Ronnie's newly diagnosed "condition."

"I don't really care if he has ADHD," I griped. I was venting my frustration and wanting Bernie to validate my discontent. Instead, he came to Ronnie's defense.

"You know, you've been in the marriage a long time," he counseled. "And he has this condition. You really oughta care about it."

I was annoyed. This was not what I wanted to hear— especially from Bernie.

He was lying on the bed and asked me to come over and give him a back rub. "Why don't you come over here and give me a massage," he said. He was clothed at the time.

"No," I told him. "I don't like giving massages." This was not the reason I was refusing. I didn't like the tone he used. It didn't have enough of a request in it. It wasn't like he was ordering me, but it felt like an order. It sounded more like he was talking to the hired help and not making a request from one lover to another.

"Especially the kind you prefer," I added. Bernie had told me about his little pastime. He indicated that he liked his massages "deep and painful." He said the masseuse indicated there was a psychology behind people who enjoyed that type of pain. I was not interested in that particular kind of interaction. Giving Bernie a massage would have made me feel cheap.

He backed off easily. He simply said, "Okay," when I told him I wasn't interested.

That night, we made love for the second time. When Bernie got up to use the bathroom, I caught a glimpse of him in the buff. It looked like the circumference of his penis was small enough that it would easily fit inside the opening of a single-serving honey jar like the one sitting on our room-service tray. On the bright side, oral sex would be a breeze.

"I used to get harder when I was younger," Bernie told me when he came back to bed.

"I wish we could be together more," he said as we lay cuddling.

"When are we going to get a chance to go away?" I asked. After nineteen years of marriage, I was looking forward to traveling, seeing the world, and enjoying a whirlwind romance.

"Sheryl, I don't think that's going to happen. I'm not allowed to travel alone. I'm not to be trusted."

"What do you mean, you're 'not to be trusted'?"

He shrugged and gave me a look that resembled one of a child telling his friends he was grounded.

"Why?"

"I wasn't so well behaved in my younger days, when Ruth and I lived on Long Island. I kept an apartment in the city and often stayed there when I worked late. Somehow, Ruth suspected there was something going on."

Bernie told me of his wild nights out on the town with his Wall Street buddies. He was taking women dancing at the Persian Room, the once legendary nightclub in the Plaza Hotel. "I guess you could say it got a little out of hand. After a while we came to a silent agreement that I wasn't going to travel alone. If I go anywhere for more than a night or two, Ruth comes with me."

"Did you ever discuss your extracurricular activities with Ruth?" I asked.

"No, we never discussed them. It was something that was just understood. The funny thing is, I haven't lived my life like that for many years." Bernie took my hands in his, something we rarely chanced in public. "I'm serious, Sheryl. You're different. I'm not playing around with you. I care about you."

Now I realized why he and Ruth had moved to the city once their boys were out of high school. Ruth needed to keep her eye on Bernie. If Ruth suspected infidelity, then her desire to keep her husband close made perfect sense. Obviously, the fantasy affair I had hoped to have with Bernie would not be possible. I had this whole picture of us stealing away to Europe, staying in five-star hotels, and dining at five-star restaurants. Now it was clear we weren't going anywhere.

I hadn't expected that Bernie would allow himself to be so restricted. He traveled all over the world with Ruth. They were out of town at least 50 percent of the time. Yet being without Ruth for lunch or dinner took a lot of explaining, not to mention logistical planning. After all, Ruth worked at the company. She was everywhere: at the office, at home. Bernie didn't have the latitude to move freely during the daytime. The nights were almost impossible.

I saw Bernie again at the Hilton Hotel on New York's Avenue of the Americas. Since I no longer wanted someone else aware of our "soirees," as he referred to our affair, I was making the reservations, and Bernie was reimbursing me. Sometimes I wouldn't ask for the money. I was all for equality.

Making the reservations meant I had the room key and could arrive first to shower and freshen up. I'd pour myself a vodka on the rocks from the minibar, and then smoke a joint to relax. The smell of marijuana hung in the air when Bernie arrived that night.

"Oh, you smoke?" he commented. "Ruth does, too. She buys her grass from someone at the firm." I was surprised; I had no idea if he was making this up or telling the truth.

Bernie looked stressed and announced that he wanted to take a bath. "I had a hard day on the trading floor," he said. (I guess it's exhausting pretending to make all those trades.) It struck me as odd, a man in his mid-fifties sitting in a bathtub. Bernie indicated that he often took baths; water soothed him. I had already showered and wasn't getting into a bathtub with him. Even if I'd wanted to, we'd never have fit. As he sat and soaked, I lit one of the tea candles I'd brought and sat down on the edge of the tub.

We spent the next fifteen minutes talking, with me splashing him playfully. After he got out of the bathtub, he asked if I would mind if he smoked a cigar.

"You mean like my uncle Izzy?"

"Your uncle Izzy?" Bernie looked mystified.

"Yes. My uncle Izzy smoked cigars."

"Never mind. I won't smoke." Bernie smoked Davidoff cigars. But he wouldn't smoke them around me. I guess he didn't want to be compared to Uncle Izzy.

In spite of our age difference (Bernie was fifty-five then, eleven years older than I was), he was always trying to be "hip." One evening, we were listening to music in our suite at the Lowell. We often listened to music and occasionally slow-danced together in the room. A Stones song came on the radio.

"I went to a Rolling Stones concert once," Bernie boasted.

"Stones." I laughed.

"What?" he asked, puzzled.

"You went to a Stones concert, Bernie. Nobody says, 'I went to a Rolling Stones concert.' They say, 'I went to a Stones concert.'" I enjoyed teasing him.

For many years, Bernie and I would speak on December 31. We made it our business to wish each other a happy New Year. We always said we would think of each other at midnight. He told me that historically he and Ruth celebrated New Year's Eve with the same couples every year.

That year, Ronnie and I rang in the New Year with

friends at our country home in Connecticut. Life had gotten somewhat easier now that Ronnie was on medication. The medication took away the volatility and the irritability. He wasn't getting angry as often and upsetting me. Another side of him was coming out. He was sweet and good-natured. It was a side of him I loved. I jokingly referred to him as my "second husband" to our close friends. Ronnie liked hearing me say that.

My forty-fifth birthday was fast approaching; January 19 was less than three weeks away, and I reminded Bernie of the date. "I'd appreciate your remembering and calling to wish me a happy birthday," I told him. I expected to hear from him, even though I knew I probably wouldn't be seeing him that day.

To celebrate, Ronnie took me to dinner at Harry Cipriani, the fashionable Italian restaurant in the Sherry-Netherland hotel. I'd been there for drinks with Bernie. I loved their peach Bellinis. The restaurant was on the corner of Fifth Avenue and Fifty-ninth Street, across the street from the Plaza Hotel. Its interior décor was modeled after the original Harry's Bar in Venice, just off the Piazza San Marco.

I was feeling conflicted when I arrived at the restaurant that evening. I was all dressed up and on Ronnie's arm, yet disappointed that Bernie had not yet called. As we followed the maître d' to our table, I thought I recognized a few faces. I was just beginning to put two and two together when I heard someone yell, "Surprise!" Ronnie had invited ten of our friends for a surprise party.

Earlier that week, he had bought me a beautiful watch. I'd told him what I wanted, and indicated that I didn't want to pay for it. He got my drift and cashed one of his bonus checks so that the watch wouldn't turn up on our credit card statement. I felt a little guilty that I was allowing my disappointment over Bernie's failure to call interfere with the wonderful evening Ronnie had planned.

To my surprise, Benjamin Netanyahu (the man who would later twice become Israel's prime minister) was dining at Cipriani that evening. I'd been introduced to him through my work with Hadassah. I walked over to his table to say hello.

The next day, I received an apologetic call from Bernie. He said a friend of his who had been the best man at his wedding had died. There was no way for me to confirm it; I had to believe him. He was going to be in town only a few more days. He made time to see me that Friday for lunch. He'd stopped at Tiffany on his way to the restaurant and was carrying the signature blue box with the white bow when he arrived at the Plaza. Inside was a pin. It was a silver and ebony art deco bow.

"Does this mean we're pinned?" I joked.

Bernie laughed. "They showed me pens."

"It's better than a pen, Bernie."

Bernie admired the watch that Ronnie had given me. "I like to collect watches," he said.

"Oh, Ronnie has a cousin who collects watches." Bernie and I enjoyed a delicious lobster lunch. It turned out to be a delightful belated birthday celebration.

After lunch, Bernie grabbed a cab. We were standing together on Fifth Avenue when he whistled loudly. There was something about the moment that I found unusually sexy. Here was this jet-setting financier with the street skills to be able to go out and whistle for a cab.

The next time I saw Bernie I was with Ronnie. We were at a movie theater in Midtown waiting to see *Six Degrees of Separation* when I spotted him on line behind us. Bernie was a real movie buff, although he said he didn't like movies like *Schindler's List* that showed suffering and painful situations. But then again, who does? He was with Ruth and several friends. He was deeply tanned and wearing a gorgeous off-white leather jacket. He always dressed beautifully. I nodded to him imperceptibly, and he nodded back. I thought that was it. The next thing I know, he's standing there introducing himself to Ronnie. It was a defensive move. There was now no need for me to go over to him. He had effectively removed any chance of having to introduce me to Ruth. I was beginning to see that everything Bernie did was calculated.

"You've done so well for us," Ronnie told Bernie. "I really appreciate it."

Ronnie and I went inside the theater. He went to get popcorn while I went to find seats. I had just sat down near the aisle when suddenly there was Ruth and two friends excusing themselves to get past me. Of all the aisles, she chose to sit in mine. I almost freaked out. Thankfully, one of the couples got up and moved closer to the screen. Ruth went to sit in the balcony. Bernie wasn't with her. He must have gone to get popcorn, too.

Of course, I was curious. I watched as she made her way up the aisle. She didn't carry herself in a particularly feminine fashion. She appeared stiff, almost masculine, as she climbed the stairs to the balcony in search of a seat.

Bernie later expressed surprise at Ronnie's appearance. "You didn't tell me your husband was so handsome," he said. "I look like an old man compared to him."

"No you don't, Bernie." I never know what to say when people comment on Ronnie's looks. It's packaging, only a matter of luck.

Chapter Twelve

I guess what the evil genius of his scheme is and, again, I don't know when it was legit and when it became a Ponzi scheme, he's obviously showing great returns for people and then they are showing great returns to their friends so it's great advertising about him. I initially had nothing to do with there, but I started to hear about people getting really good returns so I was interested, as other people were, in making good returns, it was almost like a reward to be able to be allowed to invest with him.

—former Madoff trader Adam Cohen, speaking to CNBC
　　in 2009

It was early 1994 when Bernie told me that he and Ruth were buying a house in Palm Beach. Supposedly, the home had once belonged to a member of the Pulitzer publishing family. It was on Florida's Intracoastal Waterway, about one mile from the exclusive Palm Beach Country

Club, where he and Ruth were members. It was there that Bernie could rub elbows with members of Florida's wealthy elite.

We were walking by Rockefeller Center when I overheard him talking to his real-estate agent on the phone. Bernie was one of the first people to have a cell phone. He told me he was buying the house because Ruth felt a man of his stature shouldn't have his grandchildren sleeping in the laundry room of their Florida condominium. It sounded pretentious, but Bernie insisted his wife was not that way. He was proud of her simplicity: he said she was not into designer clothing or fancy trappings, although from everything I've read, that doesn't appear to be the case.

I was keenly aware that Ruth and Bernie lived a life of grandeur. Their penthouse apartment on Sixty-fourth Street was so enormous they had a floor plan drawn up to map the exact and correct positioning of all of its furnishings. Some time after they'd purchased the apartment, he and Ruth bought the one directly below them and turned the sprawling penthouse into a duplex.

One afternoon, I got an idea of just how much money they were spending. Bernie and I were talking about the renovations Ronnie and I were considering for our apartment on Seventy-second Street. Bernie advised me of the importance of soliciting quotes from more than one contractor. "I received quotes ranging from seventy-five to one hundred and twenty-five thousand dollars to do my den," he said.

Bernie was an enigma. He was spending hundreds of thousands, perhaps millions, of dollars on renovations. Yet earlier that month he'd complained about how much he'd paid for toys for his grandson at a fund-raiser at FAO Schwarz, the toy store on Fifth Avenue. He loved to talk about all of the fund-raisers and charitable events he was attending and in the next breath would bemoan his hectic social calendar. "I wish I could just sit in my shorts, eating a bowl of cereal and watching TV," he once said. I don't know if it was true, or if it was just his way of boasting about the many functions he was attending.

Bernie and I continued to meet whenever he was in town. For some reason, we never returned to the Lowell once we started having sex. A lot of our trysts took place at the New York Hilton. We were always playful when we were together. Bernie had soft, wavy hair, and I loved running my fingers through it and making it puffy. "Do you have a comb?" he asked one evening. He was standing in front of the mirror fixing his lapel when he noticed what I'd done to his coif. Bernie was always impeccably groomed; he went for regular manicures and pedicures and frequent trims at an upscale salon.

Pointing to my own wild mane, I said, "Does this hair look like a comb has gone through it?" We both giggled.

Bernie was a bit of a curmudgeon. Sometimes he complained of being tired or that he'd hurt himself while out "dancing" or doing manual labor around the house. I think it was an excuse so there were no expectations. "Don't expect anything too wild and crazy from me tonight," he'd say. "I was painting a yellow line on the steps outside my house in Montauk and I pulled my back out."

Our lovemaking sessions were more dynamic when I took the lead. Bernie did not take the role of aggressor in bed, although in the outside world he was very much the aggressor. I felt that this man didn't reveal himself to others. He didn't appear sexually sophisticated. He didn't really care about special lingerie. He said it was me he was interested in. He was obviously worried about the size of his penis, or he wouldn't have mentioned it to me that day on the phone.

One night after making love, still a little out of breath, he said, "You're going to kill me." I was puzzled because although it was wonderful, I wouldn't have called our lovemaking wild and crazy. "Now I know you're getting old," I said, teasing him. I was joking, but his voice took on a more serious tone. "I don't mean physically," he said. I was still lying on top of him, and his hands gently stroked my back. "I mean emotionally. You're going to kill me emotionally. I care about you too much."

Another time, as we lay in bed warm with afterglow, Bernie, in his low, rasping voice, said, "Sheryl, you're so beautiful . . . like an angel." When he saw that I was about to object, he put his finger on my mouth to quiet me. "Even without makeup, you're beautiful."

I sat up to get out of bed, and he reached for me. Tracing his hand along the curves of my naked body, he whispered, "Your sensuality is God-given. It doesn't come naturally to everybody."

I took the comment to mean that Ruth wasn't particularly sensual. He'd said it in such a sorrowful way. I think he wanted Ruth to be more independent, more eclectic in her interests, more self-confident. Personally, I think he found her boring. I think passion was lacking. To anybody married a long time, new is new and exciting is exciting. Bernie and I met right before he turned fifty. He was fifty-five when we had the affair.

During our hotel "dates," we would sit close together on the couch. He was in his boxers; I was in a little dark-green chemise. We never really got exotic. One night, however, I showed up with a bottle of Rush. I knew that men used it as a sexual enhancer and thought trying it could be fun. Bernie got a little upset when I pulled it out. "Stuff like that will give me a heart attack," he said, scowling.

Once Bernie and I started having sex, I continued to notice behaviors that I found disconcerting. He always blinked with that nervous tic. I noticed he did it more often when he was with me in private. It was easier to overlook these types of eccentricity from a person of his power and standing. But when we made love it wasn't just his eyes that twitched. There were times when his entire body shuddered. Once he settled into the lovemaking, it wasn't as severe, and it no longer startled me. Still, it was odd to have someone's whole body hiccup like that while making love.

We were in a cab one evening when I raised the issue.

I asked if maybe he had Tourette's or some other type of neurological problem.

He was indignant. "No, I don't," he insisted. "I probably jumped because you hurt me when you touched me." I knew I hadn't. But I didn't want to enter into a long discussion. Obviously, the conversation was making him uncomfortable, and I didn't want to make it any worse. I didn't want to argue with him. I liked this man and wanted to respect his privacy.

Bernie indicated that he'd never been to a psychiatrist. The closest he'd ever come to a psychological evaluation had been during a flirtation he was having with a female friend. She was a psychologist, and they saw each other on social occasions. He told me she once said he was "too sick" to have an affair with. I never asked him what prompted her to make such a statement, and he didn't offer any further comment. It sounded like she had picked up something about him over the course of their friendship. She was trained to pick up cues in people, I wasn't.

Bernie was neat. He always hung his coat in the closet and took great care with his clothing. There was one instance when he did exhibit behavior that I mistook for a phobia. He was thirsty and looking around the hotel suite for a glass to drink some water. I watched as he picked one up and examined it carefully. At first, I thought he was looking for lip prints to indicate whether I had used the glass. But then I saw him sniff it.

"What are you doing? Are you worried about drinking from my glass?" I giggled.

"No, don't be silly. I just wanted to make sure there was no alcohol in it," he explained.

I was downing vodkas pretty good back then. I knew Bernie didn't like to drink, but it was becoming clearer and clearer that he was fearful of swallowing even one drop of alcohol. I wondered what that was about, but I didn't see a need to question him further. Now, looking back, perhaps he was on some sort of medication that didn't mix well with alcohol or, more probably, he worried that "loose lips sink ships."

Chapter Thirteen

It was toward the middle of our affair when Bernie professed his love for me. We were at the Hilton Hotel and near the end of our evening together. Usually, we'd spend three or four hours talking, eating, and making love. I was getting myself together and Bernie was already dressed and pulling his coat from the closet. He was about to walk out the door when suddenly he turned back to look at me. "Sheryl, you know I love you."

I cared for Bernie tremendously. But I didn't love him. I knew there was going to be no second act to this relationship. He was never going to leave Ruth. And I was married to Ronnie. Our eyes locked, and my lips spread in a broad smile. "Good night, Bernie," I whispered.

After he left, I sat there for a while savoring the feeling. I was forty-five and at the top of my game. I had a great job. I was traveling, meeting world leaders, and I had a very powerful man absolutely gaga over me. I felt empowered. He'd just told me he loved me. Our connection was providing me with a sense of confidence and self-esteem. For a moment, I let myself imagine what it would be like to be with Bernie. He had power and prestige, and he adored me.

During one meal, he even professed his feelings about me to our server at New York's top-rated Scandinavian restaurant, Aquavit. At that time, the restaurant occupied the former town house of Nelson Rockefeller on West Fifty-fourth Street; a magnificent waterfall was the highlight of its main dining room.

"Isn't she great?" Bernie said to our waitress when she arrived to take the drink orders. "She has such control over me." I was surprised at how much he was engaging her in our conversation. Bernie was not well-known back then. But my privacy was just as important as his was. We both had significant positions. Neither one of us wanted to be found out.

Later in the meal, we were taking about the future of our relationship when Bernie surprised me with another pronouncement. "I don't deserve all I have," he announced. "I don't deserve you, either."

"Bernie, why would you say that?" I asked. I was perplexed. Self-made people usually feel that they deserve what they have because they've worked hard for it.

"I don't know," Bernie replied sheepishly. "It's just something I feel."

Sheryl and Ronnie at their wedding in 1972.
Courtesy of Sheryl Weinstein

Sheryl's college boyfriend, Joey, in 1969.
Courtesy of Sheryl Weinstein

Madoff's offices were located in Manhattan's iconic Lipstick Building.

BERNARD L. MADOFF
Investment Securities
New York □ London

MADF

Regards,
Bernie

STATEMENT OF FINANCIAL CON

Dear Sheryl, at Bache shouR
Your friend in the
in the Proper Directory love

Sheryl and Ronnie dancing at
Eric's Bar Mitzvah in 1988.
Courtesy of Sheryl Weinstein

Sheryl's son, Eric, in a school photo, in 1985.
Courtesy of Sheryl Weinstein

Sheryl with Christine Todd Whitman and an unnamed hospital liaison in her role as Chief Financial Officer at Hadassah.   *Courtesy of Sheryl Weinstein*

This photo was taken in 1993 in Washington, D.C., while Bernie and Sheryl's affair was going on. In it, Madoff appears with Richard Grasso, president of the New York Stock Exchange (left), and former Security and Exchange Commission chairman David S. Ruder (center) before the House Subcommittee on Telecommunications and Finance.   *Associated Press*

The Lowell, a quaint boutique hotel on the Upper East Side where Sheryl and Bernie had their first official "date."

The doorman and front door of Madoff's Upper East Side apartment building in Manhattan.
Fred R. Conrad/The New York Times/*Redux*

A street view of the Manhattan building where Madoff and his wife, Ruth, occupied a lavish penthouse apartment.
Patrick Andrade/The New York Times/*Redux*

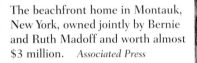

The beachfront home in Montauk, New York, owned jointly by Bernie and Ruth Madoff and worth almost $3 million. *Associated Press*

The Madoffs' multimillion-dollar mansion in Palm Beach, Florida. *Associated Press*

The entrance of Madoff's French Riviera villa, in Cap d'Antibes. *Nora Feller/The New York Times/Redux*

Bull, one of Madoff's yachts, valued at $7 million, moored in a harbor in Antibes, France.
Associated Press

The interior of Madoff's private jet.
Rex USA

Madoff in New York in 1999.
*Ruby Washington/*The New York Times/*Redux*

Bernie and Ruth at a party near Cabo San Lucas in
March 2008. *Rex USA*

Madoff enters federal court in New York on March 12, 2009. *Associated Press*

As the months passed, I began to get annoyed. There were several last-minute calls from Bernie canceling our plans. Someone had gotten him tickets to the Barbra Streisand concert at Madison Square Garden. Another time, he was on his way to Florida.

"What's the matter? What happened?" I asked. I was concerned that something was wrong. Bernie informed me that he had to be at the Palm Beach house to watch the gardener prune the trees. "What?" I asked. Perhaps I didn't understand. "Why do you need to be there?"

"Because it could take years to fix a mistake like that," he insisted.

That he was canceling a date to monitor the pruning didn't sit well with me. I didn't like playing second fiddle. Yet I knew I would never come first. I kept a close watch on my social calendar so I would never have to cancel. It was easier for me. At Hadassah, life revolved around day and evening meetings.

There had been only one time I suggested we call off a date. It was February 1994, and the New York area was being hit by a blizzard.

Bernie insisted we keep our date. When he arrived at the hotel, he shared that his son Andrew had questioned him, saying, "Who doesn't cancel a meeting on a night like this?" Of his two sons, I think Andrew was most like Bernie. He was quiet and withdrawn. I always felt Mark was more outgoing, like Bernie's brother, Peter.

While Bernie professed great love for his brother, I always wondered about their relationship.

It was around Valentine's Day when Bernie and I were having lunch at the Plaza. We were sitting in a booth at the grill on Central Park South when Bernie told me that Peter had come to him and told him he wanted to leave his marriage. He was unhappy and wanted to divorce his wife, Marion. "Madoffs don't get divorced!" Bernie was upset, and read his brother the riot act. I wasn't sure why he was sharing this information with me. Perhaps it was his cryptic way of letting me know he had no intention of ever leaving Ruth.

"If I ever left Ruth, my sons would never speak to me again," he said. "Don't you feel the same way about Eric?"

"No," I replied. "I have never felt that way. I've always felt that Eric would love me no matter what. And that he would always be there for me."

Bernie was upset the day I called his office to break our lunch date. I told him I was beginning to have negative feelings about our affair. I did not like hearing about what he and Ruth were doing, where they were going, and whom they were seeing. Their life was infinitely more fascinating than mine, and I was beginning to feel tinges of jealousy. It didn't suit my temperament.

I knew in my heart of hearts that this was never going

to be anything more than it was, simply an affair. But there was a part of me that wanted Bernie for myself. I wanted to be number one.

In the beginning, our affair was extremely titillating. Our clandestine meetings were exhilarating. There was something fun about sneaking around. We were pulling the wool over everybody's eyes. The danger was delicious, the sex heightened. We were being naughty and loving it. But after a while, it started to get old. When you have strong feelings for someone you can't be with, eventually those feelings change from pleasurable to painful. Ultimately you have to choose between the pleasure and the pain.

Bernie asked if we could meet later that evening. He wanted to see me. He didn't like hearing the word "no." We agreed to meet for drinks at the St. Moritz Hotel on Central Park South. They had a bar off the lobby. I was wearing the silvery gray charmeuse blouse he loved. He complimented me the minute I sat down at our table.

Bernie was on edge. "Sheryl, the stress is getting to me," he began. "I'm starting to feel disloyal to my wife." I didn't know if this was a defensive move on his part or if he genuinely felt this way. "People are beginning to question the way I'm behaving." I assumed he was referring to the tics. He'd been able to control them before, but now they were coming out in full force. He was ticking and blinking profusely. He was feeling more and more pressured, and it was affecting him physically. One thing I'd come to realize about him was he didn't do well with pressure.

"I understand that," I said.

"So, you think we should stop?"

"Okay," I said.

"Okay? That's it? You're being so easy on me." That was the last thing Bernie expected me to say. I don't think it went along with his perception of himself.

"Yes," I said. For the way the relationship was making me feel, it wasn't worth it. It wasn't as if I was going to move on to some glamorous life. Our affair had been something I'd tried, and now it was time to end it.

Bernie was speechless.

"I have to go now," I said. "I have to go back to the office."

"Okay. I'll talk to you soon," Bernie said. Rising from the table, he followed me out.

Ending the affair was difficult, but I was fine. This was probably the first time I'd ever done something to protect myself by not hanging on to a relationship when I should have been out the door. It was the first time I'd ever left the party while I was still having a good time.

After Bernie and I left the bar together, I went back to my office.

Ronnie and Eric were supposed to be going skiing together in a few days on Eric's spring break. When I got home that evening I learned the plan had changed. They were now heading to Cancún. The snow wasn't good in Utah. They were going to Mexico to party in the sun. It sounded like a lot of fun. I probably would have gone with them if I'd been given more notice.

Plus, Ronnie and Eric seemed eager to enjoy a father-son holiday. Ronnie's medication was doing wonders for their relationship. I didn't want to impose. It was probably better. I needed time to come to terms with the end of my relationship with Bernie.

A few days had passed when Bernie called my office. "Is there some way we can work it out?" he pleaded. "Maybe I can get away. Maybe we can go someplace."

"I don't really think there's a way, Bernie."

"Let's meet for lunch and talk about it," he implored. "I miss you, Sheryl."

It wasn't a fight. I'd given Bernie an easy out. But that didn't seem to be what he wanted. Truthfully, I don't know if Bernie even knew what he wanted.

Neither of us was leaving our marriage. As far as I was concerned, there was nothing else to say.

Part Three

Chapter Fourteen

Bernie looked for every excuse to call. A while back, I had made sure that my business interactions with him were kept to a minimum. One of my assistants at Hadassah dealt with money transfers and other requests. Ronnie and I were happy with the consistent returns we were seeing on our personal investments. Occasionally there would be losses. For the most part, though, the gains remained steady. Bernie did particularly well when there was a volatile market.

Reviewing the statements was so time-consuming that I hired someone to do it each month. When I think back on all the time and money I spent entering those fictitious trades, I feel stupid. In hindsight, Bernie probably just didn't want anybody in the office doing the programming. It would have been too labor intensive and would have required too many people being involved to generate that type of statement. I still can't believe that these fraudulent statements that can now be used as wallpaper were put out every month with imaginary trades. Not only did Bernie have no technological skills, but it must have taken a team of people to create these phantom transactions month after month, year after year. That had to be how these statements were put out while Bernie was traveling to his various homes across the country and in Europe for three weeks to a month at a time.

Sensing our affair was nearing its end, I had placed our personal accounts in the care of Bernie's right-hand man at the brokerage house, Frank DiPascali. Frank was second in command for the finance advisory part of Bernie's business. Whenever I phoned to speak with Frank to make a withdrawal or a transfer, it was Bernie who called me back. That was fine with me. I didn't want him to just disappear. I cared about him. Besides, I was never very good at endings. After all, I was still in touch with my college boyfriend, Joey.

It was spring when Bernie and I met for drinks at Harry's Bar. The dramatic wood-and-velvet lounge occupied a corner of the second floor of the Helmsley Park Lane on Central Park South. Exotic martinis like the Big Apple, a potent blend of vodka and apple schnapps, and the Lemon Drop—vodka, fresh lemon juice, and Cointreau—were on the menu. I ordered my usual red wine. Bernie had a Diet Coke.

We sat discreetly holding hands in one of the plush upholstered banquettes, quietly discussing the possibility of a rendezvous in Florida. It turned out that I was traveling to Miami to visit my best pal, Carla W., at the same time Bernie was heading south for a vacation on Fisher Island. He had his yacht, and was motoring over from Palm Beach to visit with clients. I was supposed to call him when I arrived at the hotel in Miami Beach. We'd firm up plans then.

Bernie again launched into one of his long discussions about all the interesting and important people he'd been meeting.

"I didn't realize you had such small hands," he suddenly announced.

"I have been told that I have a small mouth, too."

"I never noticed that," he said.

I smiled at him in a telling way. He got the message, and nervously cleared his throat. It was a dig. But every once in while I liked to bring him back to earth when he was becoming too full of himself.

I had a reservation at the Fontainebleau, the fabled oceanfront resort on Collins Avenue. After checking in, I called Bernie to touch base. He was having a hectic day. Ruth had flown back to New York. Their daughter-in-law had just given birth to another grandchild. But Bernie couldn't immediately get away. He was "entertaining" a client. The client had fallen while attempting to board his boat. He was hurt and needed medical attention.

Bernie owned a fifty-five-foot wooden fishing boat that he had named *Bull*. Rybovich & Sons, famous the world over for building top-notch and luxurious vessels, had built the yacht in 1969. Bernie paid $462,000 when he bought it in 1977. (According to news accounts, the boat was always maintained and was in immaculate condition when the Feds confiscated it in early 2009.)

Bernie didn't arrive at my hotel until late that afternoon. He had a cold and was feeling under the weather, so I called down for some tea. We spent time in the room talking. He told me about the accident that had occurred earlier in the day. Clambering aboard the purpose-built sport-fishing boat could be difficult, especially for some of his older clients.

Somehow we got into a discussion about his own near-fatal boating accident. Bernie insisted his Rolex watch had saved his hand and his life when he was out on the waters alone one day and fell overboard. The motor cut his left hand, but the watch prevented the blades from slicing the veins in his wrist. What really saved him was that he had been a swimmer and was able to swim to shore. He told me he had made promises, I assumed to God, when he was swimming to shore. He didn't tell me what they were. Bernie was impressed with the size of his yacht. He once bragged that his boat was bigger than that of the king of Spain, whom he'd apparently sat near at a dinner during one of his Europeans jaunts. I reminded him that the king probably had a fleet.

I hadn't been in the sun in a while, and my legs were pasty white. To make them appear less so, I had slipped on a pair of nude stockings beneath my shorts. I never expected Bernie to try to romance me. But suddenly he reached out and started caressing my thigh.

"What do you have on?" he asked, taken aback when he realized he wasn't touching flesh.

"Stockings," I admitted, going on to explain about my pale legs.

"My wife uses a self-tanning cream."

"I've tried that. I don't turn a good color."

That's as far as we went that day. I guess if I hadn't had the stockings on, we could have gone further. Bernie and I took a leisurely stroll along the beach. It was getting late when I walked him to the parking lot. He'd driven over in his Mercedes station wagon, and had to catch a ferry back to Fisher Island. I hated to say good-bye.

I was having a hard time dealing with our breakup. The decision to end our physical affair did not end our friendship. Even after we called it quits, Bernie and I continued to get together and speak on the phone as we had in the past. Our emotional connection remained strong. Still, I found it difficult to hear about what he and Ruth were doing.

I was depressed. Our affair had gone on for some time, and for the last few years I'd had something to look forward to, a little excitement. My attempts to put it behind me were proving difficult. Bernie never really left me; we just stopped having sex, which made for less pressure, less conflict, and less excitment. To help me get over the hump, I'd begun taking antidepressants. The medication had sexual side effects, which nobody told me about, and it was more difficult to achieve orgasm during sex with my husband and my libido virtually disappeared. My therapist also failed to tell me how hard it would be to get off the medication. When I was finally ready to cut back the dosage, I suffered severe symptoms of withdrawal. It was around this time that I decided to leave Hadassah.

Ronnie met me in Florida later in the week. We spent the night at the Fontainebleau. The next day, we rented a car and drove to Boca Raton. We checked into the Marriott at Boca Towne Center, and spent several days visiting with friends in Boca, and with my in-laws in Boynton Beach. It was a pleasant trip, and Ronnie and I got along. The antidepressant I was taking sort of rounded all my corners.

Once back in New York, I had a suite at the Hilton for the Hadassah convention. Bernie and I were planning to meet at the hotel and go out for dinner. Bernie was always afraid that Ruth was going to find out. Looking back, perhaps she knew what was going on—and I don't necessarily mean with me. You can't get divorced if somebody can blow the whistle. Once divorce is on the table, the parties want the "books" opened up. Maybe it was that fear that was keeping everybody in the Madoff family in check. What else could Bernie have been so afraid of?

I asked Bernie if he'd told Peter about us. "Of course not," he retorted. "How can I tell him not to get a divorce and then talk to him about my having an affair?" When Bernie first told me about his conversation with Peter, I'd assumed he'd counseled his brother to stay in his marriage for moral reasons. Now, in hindsight, it seems more likely that business reasons played a more significant role.

After dinner, we were in my room when I teasingly pushed Bernie onto the bed. He quickly jumped up. "I can't be on the bed with you," he blurted out.

"Well, then why are you here?"

Bernie was conflicted. He was having a guilt attack. For some strange reason, the more he felt for me, the guiltier he felt about Ruth and the family. "I just thought we could fool around a bit," he said. It was as though he was trying to roll our relationship back to our courtship days. He didn't want to give up what we had, yet he was cracking under the pressure. I was about to say something when an ear-splitting sound pierced the air. It was the fire alarm. We looked at each other in disbelief.

"What do we do?" I asked.

"We'll just sit here. Maybe it's a false alarm."

It was scary. Bernie and I remained frozen on the couch. The pounding of the fire bell was deafening. I could hear doors slamming in the hallway and people rushing toward the fire exits. "Are we going to just sit here and fry?" I asked.

Eventually, everyone was allowed back into the building. Bernie and I could have become crispy critters if there had been a real fire.

Our night at the Hilton was the last time Bernie and I were ever in a hotel room together. I was trying to do something healthy by getting out before our relationship became destructive. I was attempting to find a way to maintain a business relationship and a friendship. Bernie was still talking about finding a way to make it work. When we next met for lunch at Shun Lee Palace he took me in his arms and kissed me. It was hard for both of us.

We were at the Plaza having lunch when Bernie again raised the possibility of our going away together. "Bernie, do you want me to turn you inside out emotionally?" I asked pointedly.

A terrified expression swept across his face. For a moment, he sat speechless, staring at me blankly.

"Well, I will," I threatened.

Bernie backed off at that moment. But he didn't give up.

Even after we agreed to stop sleeping together, it wasn't as if we could stop seeing each other. We'd been together for years; we had an intimate friendship and we truly cared for each other. For one thing, Bernie's firm was still handling my investments, and things were going quite well. On a personal level, I saw no reason for our friendship to end. Bernie might have annoyed me from time to time, but truthfully, I had nothing but good memories.

I trusted him one hundred percent.

Chapter Fifteen

Eric had been accepted to Cornell University for the spring semester, and I'd talked him into transferring for the second half of his freshman year. He was happy at Emory University, although he wasn't finding the course-work particularly challenging. I believed he would find a more well-balanced college experience at the Ivy League university in Ithaca, New York.

That summer, Bernie arranged for Eric to work at his brokerage firm. He was doing a little bit of everything, watching the traders and lending a hand when there was work to be done. Eric didn't care for the "good ol' boys" atmosphere. He was still very young, and it didn't suit his temperament. But Bernie was fond of him. He told me my son worked hard and was always eager to help and learn. Bernie invited him and a guest to accompany him to a black-tie affair a few weeks after Eric started with the firm. Eric enjoyed himself immensely. I was a little bit jealous. When I asked Eric how the evening went, like a typical teenage boy he offered little information.

Bernie's firm was still operating from the seventeenth and eighteenth floors of the Lipstick Building when Eric was there for his summer internship. It was only later that Bernie expanded his operations to include the nineteenth floor. All the legal operations were on the eighteenth floor, and as we now know, he was operating the Ponzi scheme from the seventeenth floor.

I was attending a meeting of Hadassah's finance advisory board in the fall of 1995 when some of the members again raised concerns about Bernie's investment practices. Every three or four months, they would review his results and see how great he was doing for Hadassah. The returns and investments were consistently good and that made budgeting for the not-for-profit organization easier. But there were always questions. The fund had become quite significant and new members were less willing to entertain Bernie's "no talk" stipulation. Because of the consistency of his game, they were implying that maybe Bernie's methods weren't quite kosher.

At that time, about 10 percent of the volume on the New York Stock Exchange was apparently going through Bernie's firm. His stock picks and his timing were impeccable, as if he had a crystal ball and could see into the future. Nobody could figure out how he was doing it. Again, speculation that Bernie might be "front-running" was tossed around. I came away from the meeting feeling upset and defensive.

Before the weekend, I instructed my secretary to call Bernie's office to make the arrangements for a meeting. I was sitting outside with friends on my deck in Connecticut when Bernie called. It was unusual for business associates to call me at home. But this was typical Bernie. He even left me his home number to call him in Montauk.

My stomach dropped when Ruth answered the phone, but I asked to speak to Bernie. I think for him it was a little thrill, having the woman he'd had an affair with call and speak to his wife. "What's the meeting about?" Bernie pumped. "Who's going to be there?"

Bernie had no problem calling me wherever I was. I was annoyed one evening when he called my apartment in the city and he got Ronnie on the phone. I wasn't at home, and Ronnie joked, "Well, maybe somebody's getting lucky." I cringed when Ronnie told me how they'd shared a chuckle over the flippant remark.

It was nearing the fall of 1995 when I went to the Lipstick Building for a meeting with Bernie and the members of the finance advisory board. Frank DiPascali was already in the conference room when I arrived that morning. It was the first time I had met him in person. Frank and I had a cordial relationship. He'd always been pleasant, and I had no complaints. But I later heard from other investors that he could be a real SOB. It appears that one of his roles at the firm was to intimidate investors who questioned Bernie's investment strategies. If you weren't "happy," you could take your money elsewhere.

His aggressive, take-it-or-leave-it attitude worked on most people. They were afraid that the firm wouldn't continue investing for them. Apparently, it was Frank's way of bullying investors to back down.

It felt strange being back in the conference room after all these years. This was where it all began. This time, I sat with my back to the view, and patiently waited for the board members to arrive. There were four or five in attendance that day. They were all prominent and credentialed people in the world of finance. They were among the top in the field, many with significant personal fortunes.

Bernie was at the meeting that day, but it was Frank who did most of the talking. He had a heavy New York accent, but he came across as very knowledgeable when he described the technique the firm was using to invest Hadassah's funds.

The board members left the meeting satisfied with what they had heard. Once again, Hadassah's funds remained with Bernie's firm.

Interestingly, one of the board members who was an investor with his own firm, and had invested for Hadassah in the past, had attended that meeting. He later tested Bernie's investment technique with some of Hadassah's money through his own channels. With results in hand, he told the board that he could not replicate Bernie's rate of returns. To me at the time, that meant he wasn't as talented as Bernie. He didn't have that unerring timing or feel for the market. The board felt the same way and stopped using him as an investor, giving the money to another firm. In hindsight, he was the honest one. After all, he wasn't making up results out of thin air.

Much later, I told Bernie about the implications and comments made by some of the board members. He didn't appear the least bit bothered. In fact, he didn't show any outward concern. Instead, he insinuated that some of those very board members were either invested in his firm or had been to his office to invest on behalf of a client. I was both surprised and perplexed. If they were investing with Bernie, or trying to become investors, then why raise concerns and make innuendos? It didn't make any sense.

"Why would you agree to let them invest when I am telling you that this is what they are saying about you?" I asked.

"They're jealous," Bernie said with a shrug of his shoulders.

I found it very stressful. I wanted to defend Bernie. But I didn't want to get in the middle. In the end, I interpreted his lack of concern to mean business is business. And I let it go at that.

Earlier that year, there had been a change of guard at Hadassah. Marlene P., our former treasurer and the woman I'd traveled to Paris with in 1992, was the newly elected president of the organization. I'd always liked Marlene, and at first, our working relationship was fine. But after years of trying to keep all those volunteers at bay, and stop them from spending too much (it's so easy to spend other people's money), I was beginning to experience burnout. The psychological machinations at Hadassah were starting to feel very similar to other destructive patterns in my life.

After thirteen years as CFO, I was looking around for something else to do. Ronnie had started a magazine that past fall and I was going to be the publisher. He'd made the job sound like taking candy from a baby. It was going to be so easy; I would be able to make a nice living and go into semiretirement.

I announced my resignation on January 19, 1997 (my forty-eighth birthday), at a midwinter meeting in New Jersey, at a Radisson hotel by Newark Airport. We were all leaving after the conference to go to Israel. I continued on at Hadassah until March 31. I then moved to my new offices downtown. I soon learned that Ronnie had done very little research before deciding to become the owner of a commercial laundry trade publication. The magazine was already in trouble when he asked me to step in. It was disappointing. But I was determined not to let it fail.

When I left Hadassah, I had accrued a lot of benefits. I had two to three years' salary coming to me as severance, and I put as much as I could into the account we had with Bernie. Ronnie and I didn't live big. We always lived below our means. Our savings had begun as my salary started increasing. What Ronnie and I had was the result of a lifetime of working hard. We had to pay for tuition for private school from the time Eric was small. Plus, he was a kid in the city and he went to sleepaway camp.

We were both extremely pleased that even during periods when the market seemed to take a hit, our investments with Bernie remained safe and steady.

After I left Hadassah, it became harder for Bernie and me to see each other. We no longer had a viable reason to get together. In the past, Bernie had always told Ruth he was meeting with the "Hadassah ladies." He no longer had that excuse. I missed our times together, the anticipation, the excitement, and the emotional connection. Our relationship gradually changed over time. Bernie and I saw each other less, but still kept up with each other. He called me every once in a while to let me know he was thinking of me. And I still felt comfortable calling him when I needed advice. When we could, we met for lunch or dinner. At one point, he confided that he had a platelet issue. He told me he'd had a blood test and his platelet level was "off the charts." He told me he made promises to God, and I think they were about us. His platelets cleared up. I believe the problem was caused by the supplements his wife was giving him. They had interfered with his blood counts. I think he was always expecting to be punished. I was disturbed that he was trying to blame our relationship for his medical concerns.

"Don't make me a reason for something bad happening," I told him.

The downside of stopping our physical affair was that I had so much pent-up passion—such raw emotion and no outlet for it. One evening while Bernie and I were having dinner at the Park Lane hotel, I talked with him about how frustrated I was.

"How do you deal with that lack of passion? Don't you miss it?" I knew he had to share some of those feelings.

Pulling a little book from his jacket pocket and smiling, he turned to a page. The first entry that caught my attention was "MIA." It had a phone number beside it. I thought he had found a girl named Mia to be his new "outlet." As it turned out, MIA stood for Miami.

"Every time I go to Miami, I have someone to call. She helps me out with that 'lack of passion.'" Bernie could tell me everything he couldn't tell his wife. I felt he was being a little bit of a show-off. He had a lot of cities listed on that page. There were at least ten or twelve abbreviated city names with numbers beside them. *Fitting*, I thought, *for a man who travels so much.* "I also have someone who comes to my home a couple of times a week for a massage. I can arrange for someone for you, too."

As far as I could tell, he spoke with sincerity, as if he really wanted to help me. But I didn't know until that moment in our relationship about the gentleman's massages he liked, otherwise known as those with "happy endings."

He inferred that the masseuse brought him to orgasm. I was taken aback at his suggestion of arranging for "professional" help for me.

"No, Bernie, I don't want you to arrange anything for me."

"Well, let me know." He smiled, tucking the book back into his jacket pocket. "If you're asking if I'm sleeping with anyone else, the answer is no. I told you before, Sheryl, that's not what I'm about anymore. You came into my life, and the intensity of my feelings for you caught me off guard. I didn't fool around for a long time before you, and now I think you've ruined me. Ruth, for better or for worse, has my loyalty. You, my dear, took what was left of my heart."

Chapter Sixteen

On September 11, 2001, I found myself running for my life in Lower Manhattan. It would be impossible to forget where I was and what I was doing when that first plane came crashing into the World Trade Center's North Tower. Ronnie and I were taking a car service to the courthouse in Lower Manhattan to answer a lawsuit relating to our business. It was a beautiful day. We had just turned off the FDR Drive and were heading west toward the courthouse area when all of sudden Ronnie said, "Look," and he pointed in the direction of the Twin Towers. His voice took on a tone of wonder because what he was seeing was the glass coming off the building, millions upon millions of pieces of glass twinkling in the sunlight.

When I looked up, I saw this massive orange-red explosive ball appearing to blow off the top of the tower. But along with this ball there came millions of pieces of paper in the air, fluttering in the sunlight. Instead of telling the driver to turn around and go home, we started arguing. Ronnie didn't want to drive any further. He said there was going to be traffic at the courthouse. I didn't want to walk because I was in high heels. Neither one of us understood the magnitude of what had just happened. We couldn't comprehend what we had seen. After that I understood the expression "I couldn't believe my eyes." The car went a few blocks more and then we got out to walk the rest of the way. People along the way told us a small commuter plane had hit the tower. As we were walking to the courthouse, we heard an explosion and felt the vibrations. We couldn't see anything because the other buildings were blocking the view. We looked at each other, and decided it was probably the fuselage. Little did we know that it was the second tower getting hit. We reached the courthouse, just six blocks away from where the horrific scene was unfolding, and were waiting to speak to a clerk when they started to evacuate the building. Our attorney had informed us that we were to go before a judge that very morning. It turned out our case wasn't even on the docket for that date.

We ran along Church Street. It was the first and only time I felt my life was in danger. In my mind, the North Tower was just going to tip over, and who knew which way it was going to fall.

I stayed close to Ronnie as we frantically sprinted—me in high heels—down the streets of Lower Manhattan, ducking beneath scaffolding in search of a safe place to hide. At one point, we got separated and I feared I might never see my husband again. It was as if I had suddenly been transported into one of those old Godzilla movies and would end up in the lizard's mouth, my feet dangling from between its lips, if I slowed down to look behind me.

I remember thinking, *Sheryl, no matter how smart you are, you can't think your way out of this one.* It wasn't panic or desperation I was feeling; my mind immediately shifted into survival mode as I navigated the streets trying to strategize a safe way out. It was a life-changing experience and I still get startled if I hear a loud noise.

A few days later, I met Bernie at a restaurant on Fifty-third Street, around the corner from his office. It was very emotional. Over lunch, I told him how thankful I was for how secure he had made our lives. I was grateful that he was taking care of our finances.

"Don't be silly," he said. He seemed uncomfortable. I thought he was embarrassed by my praise. He seemed to want to get off the topic. Now I know why!

In recent years, Bernie had been producing returns of 8.5 to 12 and 14 percent. He did best in volatile markets because he could take advantage of the downside and the upside. With the puts and the calls, he could make money coming and going. He also seemed to always know which horse was going to win. His timing was impeccable. He sold AIG right before it tanked. What great timing. It was amazing. AIG went down to almost nothing, but we were out of it three days before, according to Bernie's trade confirmations. Obviously we now know he predated them and printed them after the fact. For us, his investors, it wasn't about the large gains, it was about the steady returns. It was such a relief that he had been smart enough to sell AIG before it collapsed.

For years, Ronnie would say to me, "People are making fortunes on the tech stocks. Why aren't we?"

I would tell him what Bernie had told me: "We're not going to hit a home run, but we're not going to strike out, either."

Most of Bernie's clients were very conservative people. People are focusing on the direct investors, and not on the indirect investors.

In 2003, I lost my mother. We had become a little distant after I discovered she had a gambling problem. It was around the time I began working at the magazine that I discovered she'd been making withdrawals from the account she had with Bernie's firm. The amounts were significant, in the tens of thousands. One year, she withdrew almost $70,000. I had no idea what was going on. Mom was living in a little condominium on Long Island. She had never been a big spender. She smoked cigarettes, and that was it.

After my father died, Ronnie and I had sent her on a trip to Israel, and she'd enjoyed it immensely. But as far as I knew, she hadn't been traveling, and I couldn't for the life of me imagine what was going on. What I soon learned was that my mother, Edie Wasserman, the book-keeper, had a gambling problem. This was her deep, dark secret.

It had started out small. After my father died, she was visiting Eric at college, and had taken to stopping off at the Indian reservation near Syracuse to gamble. Later on, she moved from putting one dollar in the slot machines to twenty-five-dollar chips. It was the thrill of it, the excitement, the action. She felt like a big *macher,* the Yiddish VIP.

One weekend, she went down to Atlantic City and won big. Suddenly she had limos picking her up at her house on Long Island, and casinos were "comping" her with hotel rooms and meals. I was crying when I confronted her on the phone. "Mom, this is not how you raised me," I pleaded. "This is not how we lived." Ronnie and I had taken such care to make sure that she was comfortable and financially secure. "Mom, everything is set up for you. You can afford to spend whatever you want, but you can't afford to just give it away."

"You're right," Mom told me. I felt relieved. I continued monitoring her account, and saw that she had stopped withdrawing money. I assumed everything was okay.

I was devastated when she was diagnosed with primary peritoneal carcinoma, also known as ovarian cancer's "wicked stepsister." It was probably the same aggressive cancer that had killed my grandmother. I didn't learn about Mom's second mortgage or her enormous credit card advances until her final hospital stay. By early 2003, her cancer had spread to the cervical area of her spine, and to two areas in her brain. She was at NYU Medical Center for palliative treatment. I feel the brain tumors had a great effect on her judgement. There was no cure at that point, but Mom didn't know that. She was trying to reach a friend to tell her to intercept her mail. She was worried I would find out the story of her finances as soon as I got to the mail. I started seeing the bills and the bank statements, and the markers started coming in. Mom had stopped taking withdrawals from Bernie, but she'd discovered Ditech.com. She had a second mortgage on her home, cash advances on her credit cards. A $15,000 marker came in the week she entered the hospital, and the markers continued even after she died.

She was a very honest woman, and keeping this secret had to have been difficult for her.

When my grandmother was dying, my mother had spent every day by her bedside in the hospital. I wanted to do the same for her. At the time, she was on morphine. I sat down next to her bed and asked if she could understand me. She said she could.

"I know all about Atlantic City and I know all about the money," I told her. "You and Daddy worked so hard for your money. You earned it, and it is yours to do what you want with. I don't need or want it for myself. I just wanted you to be happy and secure. I know people can't be happy when they're losing."

Mom was tortured. I could sense her relief once it was out in the open. She even admitted that I was right.

Thankfully, I could spend every day with her there. It brought us very close. When I needed to go into the office, Ronnie and Eric came and watched over her. Ronnie was amazing.

Mom and I had really good closure. I remember getting into her hospital bed in the spoon position and holding her. I just wanted her to know I was there. She was under heavy morphine and she died on February 19, 2003. She was seventy-six years old. She had been strong, independent, and spirited right up until the end.

My mother's gambling addiction, or perhaps the effects of the brain tumors, were something I chose not to share with Bernie. He and his family were coping with tragedies of their own.

During one phone call, Bernie shared with me that his brother Peter's son, Roger, had been diagnosed with leukemia in 2002. After enduring two years of chemotherapy and radiation, two stem-cell transplants, and numerous immunosuppressive treatments, he went on to write a book titled *Leukemia for Chickens*. Peter was terribly distraught. Roger Madoff later died from the complications of a second transplant. He was thirty-two. Bernie told me Peter was becoming more religious, and after his son's death was actually gathering minyans, ten-man quorums, and praying at the office. Bernie chuckled, which I felt was insensitive. Obviously Peter was looking for some comfort. Bernie also told me his own son Andrew had been diagnosed with mantle cell lymphoma, and his great-niece, his sister Sondra's granddaughter, also had leukemia. Thankfully, his great-niece was cured, and Andrew went into remission. In January 2008, Andrew became chairman of the Lymphoma Research Foundation, but he resigned shortly after his father's arrest that December. It was around the time his son was diagnosed and his nephew died that Bernie began telling me that he was "lacking energy." He was going to bed earlier and he wasn't going out.

"You must be feeling depressed," I said. To which he replied, "No."

I can't imagine he wasn't upset about what was going on in his family. I think depression is viewed by men as a weakness, that depression is really just a zapper of energy. In subsequent conversations, Bernie complained about getting old and bemoaned the fact that nobody cared about him. Later, when there were reports of what charities Bernie's firm had "stolen" from, the leukemia and lymphoma foundations were not among them, but Gift of Life, which dealt with bone marrow registry, was.

Over lunch one day, Bernie told me rather proudly that he'd given Peter a small piece of the business. I thought it was generous until I learned that he was talking about only 1 percent. There must have been more to this than meets the eye. But that's what Bernie gave to him.

Peter's daughter, Shana, was married for the second time in 2007. Bernie and I had shared a laugh some years back when the announcement of her first marriage had appeared in *The New York Times*. We were having dinner at the Pierre one night and he told me that his niece's wedding was going to be at the Pierre. He'd related the gist of a call he'd received from a friend commenting on Shana's title at the firm. The friend had seen her wedding announcement in the *Times* and found it amusing that a twenty-seven-year-old was Compliance Officer of Bernard L. Madoff Securities. Shana's new husband, Eric Swanson, had been a midlevel official at the SEC's Washington headquarters for ten years.

In the fall of 2007, Bernie and I had lunch at the Brasserie in Midtown. Initially, I wasn't happy about eating there because it can be noisy. Although it was only the two of us, Bernie had reserved a table for four. We had a large booth to ourselves. During the conversation, I mentioned that Ronnie and I were going on a cruise. In the last few years, Ronnie and I had begun to travel. On this trip we were flying to Thailand, and then cruising Thailand, Vietnam, and Hong Kong.

"I've never been on a cruise," Bernie lamented. Which made me smile, and laugh. "What do you mean? You have a few boats. You have your own private cruises all the time."

"Yes, well, my friends have talked about being on cruises."

"So go on a cruise. What's stopping you?"

"For some reason, things are continuing to be busy at the office. I thought I could be winding down now. But it doesn't look that way."

We started talking about the kids. He told me about how Andrew was getting separated.

"I'm sorry to hear that," I said.

"No, it's better that way," Bernie replied. "She appears to lack emotion. She's a cold fish."

"That's too bad," I said.

Bernie told me that Mark had remarried and had a daughter. The little girl was in nursery school, and she was in a recital on Yom Kippur. He and Ruth were going.

I thought, *What kind of school in the New York area has a recital on Yom Kippur?*

Toward the end of our meal we spoke a bit about Eric. I had a weighty problem that involved my son and I turned to Bernie for advice. It was one of the last things I brought up. I was very hesitant. It might have been the only time in our relationship I was able to show my need for something he had to offer. Bernie listened attentively. He told me to have Eric call him to discuss the possibility of Bernie's giving him a few people to speak to regarding certain business issues. They in fact turned out to be very useful. I was grateful. Bernie told me during lunch that it was getting really difficult for him to see me. How could he explain being out with me when I was no longer with Hadassah?

"Why don't you go work for Hadassah again?" he joked.

It was nice to see him; nice to touch base. We considered each other old friends.

My last phone call with Bernie was around his birthday in April 2008. I called to extend birthday greetings.

He told me that he was going to be away on and off for a few months in Europe. He and Ruth were taking a long vacation.

"I'll be in touch after the summer," he said.

That was the last time we ever spoke.

Chapter Seventeen

Until that fateful moment, December 11, 2008, had been a particularly good day. Earlier that afternoon, I'd entered the numbers from our latest financial statement from Bernard L. Madoff Securities into my computer and saw that we had finally gotten where we'd always wanted to be. I couldn't wait to tell Ronnie that we'd reached the financial goal we'd set for ourselves so many years before.

Ronnie and I had a trip to Florida planned for the following week. We were attending the wedding of one of my oldest friends' daughters. I couldn't wait to spend some time with my friends and enjoy the warmer weather. In preparation for the trip, I had a manicure/pedicure appointment scheduled for 5:30 that afternoon. At about 4:45 I started wrapping things up. I knew I'd be out of the office for several days, so I began gathering the files I would need into my bag.

I was about to shut down my office computer when my private line started to ring. I smiled, seeing my son's number flash on the caller ID.

"Mom, Mom, did you hear what happened to Bernie?" Eric asked. His voice was hoarse and choked with anxiety. At first I thought Bernard Madoff had had a stroke or had suffered a heart attack.

"What? What happened to Bernie?" My smile vanished as I heard the distress in Eric's voice. I was concerned but not alarmed.

"A friend just e-mailed me an article. Bernie's been arrested."

"Eric," I said, "don't overreact. A number of years ago, the SEC investigated him and found nothing, not a thing. They're always going after him. It's okay."

My words did nothing to alleviate Eric's fears. "Bernie turned himself in."

I didn't want to believe what I was hearing. It had to be a mistake. Instinctively, I tried to reassure Eric. There was no way what he was saying could be true.

"Mom, I'm going to e-mail you the article. You can read it for yourself."

I watched the computer screen as the envelope indicating new mail appeared. My hand began to shake as I used the mouse to click on the *Wall Street Journal* link. Suddenly, Bernie's picture flashed on the screen beneath a headline that read:

Top Broker Accused of $50 Billion Fraud:
Sons Turned in Madoff After He Allegedly Told
Them His Investment-Advisory Business for the
Wealthy Was "Giant Ponzi Scheme."

"Oh my God!" I sank back in my desk chair, trying to wrap my head around the unthinkable.

"There's no mistake, Mom. It was a huge scam. The money—our money—is gone," Eric groaned.

The news was impossible to grasp. It was unfathomable. Bernie had "invested" my family's money for more than fifteen years. This man had been a dear friend for more than twenty years.

"Mom, you have to fax Bernie's office right now! Mom, Mom, do you hear me? You've got to tell them to withdraw our money! Mom! Mom . . ." I could hear Eric becoming frantic through the receiver, but I was paralyzed and could barely reply.

"Honey, everything will be fine," I soothed. Although I didn't feel it, my maternal instincts took over and my first thought was, *I'm soothing my son.* "I'm going to fax the office right now," I told him. Of course, I wasn't. But he was adamant.

I needed to get my son off the line. I needed to think about what to do. At that moment, I decided to call the offices of Bernard L. Madoff Investment Securities. When no one picked up, I told myself this was not unusual. It was after five, and the offices were closed for the night.

For a fleeting moment, I contemplated dialing Bernie's cell phone. I knew the number; it was programmed into my phone. He always picked up when I called. And if he couldn't, he'd get back to me right away. I was now too afraid. What if what was being said was true? I didn't want to risk having my number show up on any call logs. Bernie was the subject of a criminal investigation, and while I knew absolutely nothing about what he'd done, I was suddenly afraid that by calling him I'd somehow be implicated.

I sat in my office; the files I'd been packing into my tote fell from my hands and fluttered across my desk. My head was exploding. Amid a rush of emotions, I thought back to that winter day in 1988 when I first met Bernard Madoff. I knew I needed to call Ronnie. As I dialed his cell phone, I felt as if I was in a trance. Ronnie was in the car on his way home from work. Though I wasn't crying, my voice was heavy with emotion. I knew there was no point in beating around the bush, so when he answered I said, "Ronnie, I have to tell you something."

"What? What's the matter?"

"Bernie was arrested. They're saying it was a Ponzi scheme."

There was a pause as the full meaning of what I had said sunk in.

"Oh my God. Oh my God. . . . Well, at least nobody died."

And really, there was nothing else either of us could say at the moment. Ronnie offered to stop by my office and pick me up. Moving on autopilot, I finished packing my bag, canceled my manicure appointment, and went downstairs to wait for him. As we made our way from my office on Fifty-seventh Street to our apartment on Seventy-second, the drive-time news reports were buzzing with the Madoff story. Sitting there listening as the reporters rehashed the emerging details and tried to relay the scope of the scandal, the out-of-body feeling grew stronger.

The irony of my having believed only an hour before that Ronnie and I had achieved our lifelong financial goal was sickening. But it really didn't matter how much we'd lost, because we'd lost everything. Everything is always too much to lose.

I laid my head back on the headrest and took a few deep breaths. I couldn't scream or cry. I just sat there with a million questions racing through my mind. *How would we survive? Where would we live? How could I not have known? Why hadn't the SEC known before now? And how could my one affair in more than thirty-six years have been with the world's biggest crook?*

At home that night, having counted up what we had left, we felt almost as if we'd experienced death. It was the death of our dreams, of what tomorrow was going to bring. What we thought our life was going to be had been wiped out in an instant. The secret I'd held close—cherished— for so long turned into a bitter poison that threatened to destroy me.

Despite the numbness, reality took hold. What we had wasn't much. I had taken a withdrawal about three months earlier, so we would have that money to pay taxes. We had one other small account, and that was it.

My income from the trade magazine we published had fallen sharply that year because our advertisers were experiencing the full brunt of the nation's struggling economy. Looking forward to retiring, Ronnie had cut back significantly on his workload. As a result, his income was also down. A few years earlier, we had refinanced our apartment and given the equity to Bernie to invest. Periodically we would make withdrawals from our investment account to subsidize our cash requirements, the mortgage payment on our apartment, as well as the payment on a second home we'd purchased in a fifty-five-and-over community on Long Island's East End. Now, without that source of income, even with both of us working, we could barely afford the two mortgages, never mind the rent on my office space.

As I sat in my living room watching news reports chronicling the story, I was finding it hard to conceive of how this had happened. Bernie's statements had been reviewed annually by the SEC and many other agencies, and yet nobody had picked up on anything suspicious? If you had asked me if this could have happened, I surely would have said no. But clearly, there is a real gap in our regulatory system. Here it was unraveling right before my very eyes.

Ronnie and I thought we had enough money for retirement. We thought we had more than we ever imagined we would. We had hit our goal. But that day we found out we had nothing but mortgages and bills. We had seven accounts, including my parents' and my son's. The adage of not putting all your eggs in one basket was not really pertinent. We thought we had a very diversified portfolio of blue-chip stocks and government bonds. The thought of theft never occurred to me. After all, how many people have more than one brokerage account?

All those years, Bernie was sending us trades and confirmations that never existed. Our money wasn't with an investment adviser but with a brokerage firm whose principal, Bernie Madoff, had been the chairman of NAS-DAQ for a number of years. He wasn't a three-card monte hustler who grabs you and pulls you into his scheme on a street corner. Then again, maybe he was but in the ulti-mate disguise.

Epilogue

When a person hears that we were victims of Bernie Madoff, the first question they ask is, "How much did you lose?" I find it an interesting as well as intrusive question. We normally don't ask people how much money they have or make, so why do so many people feel comfortable asking about the amount of the loss? Does the largeness of the amount make it more important? Does the smallness make it less important? What some people don't seem to grasp is that, in the end, it's what you're left with that matters. Trust me when I say that it's very tough to have virtually nothing left.

I knew how it happened to me, so it wasn't a matter of how this could happen but maybe why. How could Bernie have done this for such a very long time without being caught? To this day it is almost impossible for me to believe that this man I had known and cared about had stolen billions and billions and billions of dollars.

The magnitude of the crime was, and still is, incomprehensible.

Unable to accept what had happened to us, to me, I searched for some plausible explanation. Because of the way I was responding, Ronnie felt I was defending Bernie. It wasn't that I was defending him; I just didn't have those strong hateful feelings. I felt lost and confused.

Ronnie and I were in shock. Initially, it was too much to absorb. I could make up excuses for Bernie. When I first asked him to invest our personal money, he couldn't take the risk of alienating me by saying no, and if he tried to get me out later on, he couldn't take the risk of me making problems for him vis-à-vis Ruth. Not that I could ever imagine doing that, until now. But then again, why bother making excuses for the inexcusable—there is no acceptable excuse.

In retrospect it becomes fairly obvious to me that it was always about Bernie and his needs. In my mind's eye I envision him as a small boy—a child with an array of neurological issues: significant eye blinking, throat clearing, possibly a tendency to stutter, and maybe other physical traits out of the norm. I see his parents as not particularly warm or loving people—maybe embarrassed by their small son's bizarre behaviors. He spoke to me of his fear of his grandfather's "strap" (was it ever used on him?) and his need for excessive order at an early age. I have no idea what caused these fears or needs because I never asked and he didn't tell me, but they were there. I then picture him growing up and beginning to reach puberty, and having the realization that his penis was small and all the thoughts of additional embarrassments and inadequacies burdening his already damaged psyche—another of his secrets to keep hidden.

Bernie almost never spoke to me about his parents. What he did share was the pride he felt about so many of his clients viewing him and treating him as a son. He seemed to need this type of closeness and continued reaffirmation from others. Was this a form of self-healing for him because he lacked feeling that acceptance, love, pride, or closeness from his own parents growing up? Did it fulfill a need in him to feel worthy, something that may have been lacking all those formative years?

In the statement he made during the sentencing he said that he continued with the fraud because he could not accept the fact that he had failed. In other words, he couldn't admit his failure to others—so instead he continued to steal from them.

I believe that when the entire truth is made known it will be revealed that his fraud had gone on for much longer than he has admitted to. His lack of self-esteem and consequent need to preserve his successful image outweighed any other moral considerations. It will be left to the psychologists and psychiatrists to define him in more accurate or professional terms, whether it be as a sociopath or some other name. The problem with sociopaths is that you don't find out about them until it is too late.

On June 29, 2009, I was one of nine witnesses to deliver a victim impact statement at his sentencing in federal court in Lower Manhattan. I felt it was important for me to be able to face him and say how I felt. Part of me was very glad the judge had granted me permission. Another side was very apprehensive, thinking of ways I could not show up and what good excuses I could use. But in the end, I decided it was something I had to do. I felt nervous and didn't sleep well the night before.

I didn't know in what order we would be speaking but I soon found out it would be alphabetically and that I would be last. I was getting a little anxious—especially around the time we were expecting Bernie to make an appearance. When he did arrive in the courtroom, he looked like Bernie—maybe a little thinner, maybe a little grayer, but he looked like Bernie. I thought he looked a little too good for having been in prison all this time; I expected him to look worse for the wear. We didn't catch each other's eye in the crowd. In a second he sat down with his back to us. He and the entire courtroom faced the judge. As I stared at the back of his head I did make a mental note that his haircut wasn't up to his previous standards.

Finally, the judge announced my name. Ronnie and I rose and started walking toward the microphone. There was no podium. Many thoughts were going through my mind. My greatest fear was that I would suffer a sudden panic attack—that out-of-body sensation in which you feel that your voice is "floating away" and disappearing. I was also wondering what Bernie might be thinking. Was he worried that I would tell all to the world? That thought and his probable anxiety made me smile inside. Standing before the court, about to confront him—my own personal nightmare—I was not afraid. I had done nothing wrong.

With Ronnie standing beside me I made the following statement in court:

Your Honor,

I was introduced to Bernard Madoff twenty-one years ago at a business meeting. At the time I was the Chief Financial Officer of Hadassah, a charitable women's organization. I now view that day as perhaps the unluckiest day of my life because of the many events set into motion that would eventually have the most profound and devastating effect on me, my husband, my child, my parents, my in-laws, and all those who depended upon us for their livelihoods.

You have heard and you will hear from many of us—the old, the young, the healthy, and the infirm—about the unimaginable extent of human tragedy and devastation. According to a *Time* magazine article, there are over three million individuals worldwide who have been directly or indirectly affected.

They—the media and the press—speak of us as being greedy and rich. Most of us are just ordinary working people—work-a-bees, as I like to refer to us. My husband and I are now both in our sixties and have been married for thirty-seven years. We have saved for most of our lives by living beneath our means in order to provide for our retirement. This past Thursday at two P.M., my husband and I sold our home of twenty years. People are always asking, How much did we lose? My reply is that when you have lost everything it really doesn't matter because you have nothing left. And we have lost everything. Many have told us that we were lucky—I no longer know how to define lucky—to be able to sell in this depressed market, although at a greatly reduced amount. We had to sell because four years ago we refinanced the mortgage and gave the excess cash to Madoff to invest. There was very little left over after all was said and done.

It's difficult to describe how it feels to be virtually forced out of your home due to circumstances outside of your control—to leave unwillingly. Last Tuesday I walked out following the movers with the thought that I would be back before the closing but knowing in the back of my mind that I wouldn't. My husband was the last to be in our home. He shared with me his hesitation of not wanting to leave, of wanting to remain but realizing that staying was no longer an option. We chose not to go to the closing because it would have been just too painful for either of us to be there.

For months after December 11 I would wake in the dark hours of the night and early morning and, to my horror, realize that there were no calming, soothing words I could say to myself because it wasn't a dream. The monster who visited me was true, a reality. Those same thoughts would occur to me upon waking in the morning and during the day. A deep, heavy depression would surround me and not lift. This went on for many months. I walked as if in a dream, virtually unable to eat, the sight of food making me feel sick, unable to escape the reality of my personal devastation. At times I could not even bear to be alone. I would ask my friend Selita to stay with me at the office even if there was very little work to do. It would prompt me to pick up the phone to call my husband to be reassured that I was not alone.

This continued until March 12 when Madoff entered his plea of "guilty." I began to speak out to the media and the helpless and hopeless feelings began to retreat. I began to feel empowered. It came together for me while being interviewed by Katie Couric. She asked me, "Weren't you embarrassed being a CPA and losing all of my money?"

At that moment I realized and responded, "No, I wasn't embarrassed because I did not lose my money. My money was stolen from me."

Ms. Couric said to me, "You sound angry," and I said, "Yes, you're right, when somebody steals from you, you get angry." That was the beginning of my healing process.

I felt it was important for somebody who was personally acquainted with Madoff to speak. My family and I are not anonymous people to him. He knows that my husband's name is Ron and that my son's name is Eric. And in fact, Eric worked for him one summer while in college many years ago. Eric would continue to call him over the years to ask for his advice and input. Eric entrusted him with his own money that he worked for and saved. A few months before this all happened, Eric had spoken to him and thanked him for doing such a good job.

I would now like to have the opportunity to share with you my personal feelings about Madoff and to speak to his sentencing. I remember when my son was perhaps a few weeks old and I would watch him as he slept and he would whimper—not a cry of hunger, but a whimper.

Even at a few weeks old there was something in his subconscious that could frighten him. It amazed me that such a young child, an infant, could have nightmares. All of us remember those times from our earliest ages when the terror, the monsters, the goblins would visit us in those dark hours. Eventually, we would be so frightened that we would awake, sometimes calling out to our parents because we were so frightened. It was calming to have our parents remind us that it was only a dream.

As we got older, we could wake ourselves up and assure ourselves that it was only a dream. That terror, that monster, that horror, that beast now has a name to me and it is Bernard L. Madoff.

I will now attempt to explain to you the nature of this beast whom I call Madoff. He walks among us, he dresses like us, he dines and eats and drinks and speaks, but underneath the façade there is truly a beast. He is a beast who has consumed, for his own needs, the livelihoods, the savings, the lives, the hopes, the dreams and futures of others with total disregard. He has fed upon us to satisfy his own needs. No matter how much he takes and from whom he takes it, he is never satisfied. He is an equal-opportunity destroyer.

I felt it important for you to know that in appearance, he appears to be like everybody else, and it is for this reason that I am asking your honor to keep him in a cage behind bars because he has lost the privilege of walking and being among us mortal human beings. He should not be given the opportunity to blend so seamlessly into our society again.

I would like to suggest that while any man, woman, or child that has been affected by his heinous crimes still walks this earth, that Madoff the Beast should not be free to walk among them. You must protect society from the likes of him.

I have reread Madoff's March 12 statement to you. Certain quotes jumped out at me—his continuing self-serving references that his "proprietary trading and market making business managed by his brother and two sons was legitimate, profitable, and successful in all respects." Or that he felt "compelled to satisfy my clients' expectations, at any cost." It sounds as if he's laying the blame on his clients' expectations and never admitting the truth that he was stealing from these clients and the lives he ruined. If he was attempting to protect his family, he should not be given that opportunity because we the victims did not have the same opportunity to protect our families. Madoff the Beast has stolen our ability, the ability to protect our loved ones, away from us. He should have no opportunity to protect his family.

We the victims continue to be disappointed by those agencies that were set up to protect us. SIPC has now redefined what we are entitled to, the IRS approved Madoff's request to be a nonbank custodian for our IRAs and pension funds, and the SEC appears to have just looked the other way on numerous occasions.

This is a human tragedy of historic proportions and we ask—no, we implore—that those agencies that may have failed us in the past through acts of omission step up to the plate and fulfill their responsibilities.

I thank you, your honor, for your indulgence and I feel confident that you will make sure that justice is served.

Thankfully my voice was strong and clear. My confidence kicked in and my inner strength took hold and carried me through those difficult moments. I was able to speak with emotion and conviction. As I finished, there was applause in the room. Other "victims" stood and welcomed me back to my seat with hugs and thanks. I was so relieved because I felt that I was able to represent myself, as well as the many thousands of others who did not get the opportunity to speak, in a meaningful and purposeful way.

I wasn't filled with anger or hate. I felt a certain amount of sympathy for Bernie because he had no family, no friends, nobody there with him. The judge specifically spoke to that, remarking that he had not received one letter in Bernie's favor. The judge found it very telling.

For his crimes, Bernie received a sentence of 150 years in prison, the maximum allowable under federal guidelines. On July 14, 2009, he was transferred to Butner Federal Correctional Complex in Butner, North Carolina, where he will spend the remainder of his life as prisoner No. 61727-054. This doesn't really change anything for us—we are still coping with the many issues caused by his crimes and probably will for the rest of our lives. As I walked out of the courthouse I felt a sense of pride returning. I am a very private person, but I had a story to tell. I have learned that sharing empowers and does not weaken. This was part of the process of getting my voice back, as well as my self-esteem, which has taken quite a beating. I refuse to view myself as a victim. I am determined to get back to my future.

Appendix A

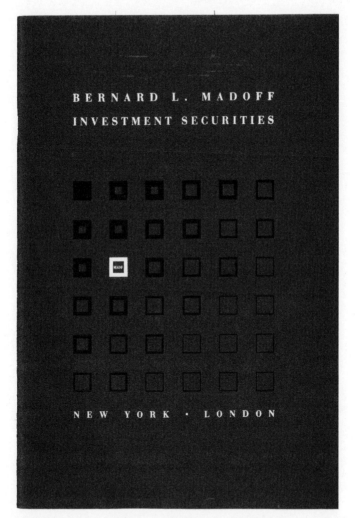

This promotional booklet for Madoff Investment Securities matched the masculine black-and-silver design of the company's offices. Both were designed to inspire a sense of confidence and security in the prospective and current Madoff client.

Appendix A

**Bernard L. Madoff Investment Securities:
A Global Leader in Trading U.S. Equities**

B ernard L. Madoff Investment Securities is the world's largest market-maker in off-exchange trading of listed U.S. equities. The firm has attained its position as a global leader because of what it does for its clients: Madoff Securities guarantees to buy or sell up to 5000 shares of any stock in the Standard & Poors 500 Stock Index (S&P 500) at the best prevailing price. It also offers clients opportunities for price improvement as well as highly competitive bids and offers on larger orders.

Madoff Securities' customers include scores of leading securities firms and banks from across the United States and around the world. The firm is not only a leading market-maker in all of the S&P 500 stocks as well as over 100 NASDAQ issues, it is also one of the largest market-makers in U.S. convertible bonds, preferred stocks, warrants, units, and rights. The firm is known for its fine pricing as well as its ability to execute most orders in seconds. Because it acts as principal in all of its transactions, Madoff Securities does not have to go to any exchange floor to find the other side of transactions. It quotes prices on a net basis.

Madoff Securities' superior service is made possible by a sophisticated dealing staff backed by the securities industry's most advanced technology. It is underpinned by the personal commitment of founder Bernard L. Madoff, his brother Peter B. Madoff, who is the senior managing director and head of trading, and Madoff Securities' team of 150 employees.

Their dedication to providing the best prices and the fastest execution has enabled the firm to become far and away the leading firm in the U.S. "third market," which trades U.S. listed equities away from the exchange floor.

Madoff Securities is a registered U.S. broker/dealer regulated by the Securities and Exchange Commission and the National Association of Securities Dealers, the leading U.S. self-regulatory organization. Madoff Securities International is a member of the London Stock Exchange and is regulated by the Securities and Futures Authority.

Since its founding in 1960, Madoff has compiled an uninterrupted record of growth which has enabled the firm to continually build its financial resources. It currently ranks among the top 75 U.S. securities firms in total capital, and it is in the top 50 in excess capital, a measure of financial strength.

Appendix A

n an era of faceless organizations owned by other equally faceless organizations, Bernard L. Madoff Investment Securities harks back to an earlier era in the financial world: The owner's name is on the door. Customers know that Bernard Madoff has a personal interest in maintaining the unblemished record of value, fair-dealing, and high ethical standards that has always been the firm's hallmark.

Bernard L. Madoff founded the investment firm that bears his name in 1960, soon after leaving law school. His brother, Peter B. Madoff, graduated from law school and joined the firm in 1970. While building the firm into a significant force in the securities industry, they have both been deeply involved in leading the dramatic transformation that has been underway in U.S. securities trading.

Bernard L. Madoff has been a major figure in the National Association of Securities Dealers (NASD), the major self-regulatory organization for U.S. broker/dealer firms. The firm was one of the five broker/dealers most closely involved in developing the NASDAQ Stock Market. He has been chairman of the board of directors of the NASDAQ Stock Market as well as a member of the board of governors of the NASD and a member of numerous NASD committees.

One major U.S. financial publication lauded Bernard Madoff for his role in "helping to make NASDAQ a faster, fairer, more efficient and more international system." He has also served as a member of the board of directors of the Securities Industry Association.

Reflecting the growing international involvement of the firm, when Madoff Securities opened a London office in 1983, it would become one of the first U.S. members of the London Stock Exchange. Bernard Madoff was also a founding member of the board of directors of the International Securities Clearing Corporation in London.

Peter B. Madoff has also been deeply involved in the NASD and other financial services regulatory organizations. He has served as a vice chairman of the NASD, a member of its board of governors, and chairman of its New York region. He has also been actively involved in the NASDAQ Stock Market as a member of its board of governors and its executive committee and as chairman of its trading committee. He has also been president of the Security Traders Association of New York.

Bernard and Peter Madoff have both played instrumental roles in the development of the fully computerized Cincinnati Stock Exchange. Peter Madoff has been a member of its board of governors and has served on its executive committee. They have helped make the Cincinnati Exchange the fastest growing regional stock exchange in the United States.

These positions of leadership not only indicate the deep interest Madoff Securities has shown in its industry, they also reflect the respect the firm and its management have achieved in the financial community.

Appendix B

BERNARD L. MADOFF
Investment Securities
885 Third Avenue New York, NY 10022-4834

212 230-2424
800 221-2242
Telex 235530
Fax 212 486-8178

March 15, 1993

Ms. Sheryl Weinstein

Hedged Equity Portfolio

Establish a portfolio of S&P 100 Index securities and hedge that portfolio by purchasing OEX index puts and selling OEX index calls.

The list of securities and the choice of strike prices of the index options will be determined by a number of circumstances, depending on our market expectations and posture, together with the current put and call premiums and implied volatility of those instruments.

In order to establish a perfect hedge, we would have to purchase all 100 securities in the S&P 100 that comprise the OEX index. Purchasing all 100 of the securities is unnecessarily costly and cumbersome, however, because the OEX is a capitalization weighted index, we can achieve a 90% correlation to the index by owning approximately 20 of the 100 S&P securities.

A key part of this strategy is to constantly monitor the hedge correlation and adjust the portfolio, by making changes to both the selection of securities, the relative weighting of each position, and the OEX strike prices.

On an annualized basis, the purchase of index puts should limit any down side loss to approximately 5%, however, the sale of index calls, the premium of which is used to offset the cost of puts, limits your maximum upside profit potential to approximately 20%.

A cardinal rule of our strategy is to never be unhedged, therefore, we will not own securities without owning index puts, nor will we sell index calls without owning securities.

Again, I reiterate that these strategies are designed to take advantage of a number of different investment climates and are not dependent solely on choosing the correct market direction. We attempt to take advantage of a combination of market volatility and price disparities, along with present option premiums and their implied volatility.

Affiliated with:
Madoff Securities International Ltd.
43 London Wall, London England EC2M 5TB.071-374 0891

Our firm is a registered market maker in all of the S&P Index securities and in that role handle approximately 10% of all the transactions in equities in the U.S. Because of this fact, we enjoy a significant cost and speed advantage in monitoring and executing these strategies, which greatly enhances our performance.

U.S. Treasury Portfolio Yield Enhancement

The goal of this strategy is to enhance the yield on U.S. treasury instruments through the sale of options, which would generate additional income from the premiums on these instruments. The current portfolio of U.S. Government Securities is analyzed to determine a weighted coupon and duration to maturity. A blend of options (on the T-Bill future, 2 year note future, and 5 year note future) allows for matching option positions with weighted long Government Securities portfolio.

Appendix C

Investment Securities
885 Third Avenue New York, NY 10022

800 221-2242
Telex 235130
Fax 212 486-8178

Bernard L. Madoff

January 13, 1995

Ms. Sheryl L. Weinstein

Dear Ms. Weinstein,

Bernard L. Madoff Investment Securities is a registered broker/dealer with The United States Securities and Exchange Commission (SEC) and The National Association of Securities Dealers, Inc. (NASD). Accordingly we are required to comply fully with the regulations of both these bodies as they relate to the custody of customer securities. We hereby confirm that all securities including U.S. Treasury instruments are held by us, for your account, as custodian in a segregated account at The Depository Trust Company (DTC). We further confirm that the securities held for your account are never loaned or pledged.

If we can be of further assistance, please feel to contact us.

Sincerely yours,

Bernard L. Madoff

BLM/ep

Affiliated with:
Madoff Securities International Ltd.
43 London Wall, London England EC2M 5TB 071-374 0891